Pearson's Canal Com...

WELSH

Published by Central Waterways Su...
Tel/fax: 01788 546692 email: sales@...
Copyright: Michael Pearson - All righ...
Seventh edition 2006. ISBN 0 954911...
ISBN-13 978-0-9-5491163-8

C000213754

Please lift your fenders

tillerman

Everybody knows that 2005 was the bicentenary of Trafalgar. Rather less well known is the fact that Pontcysyllte Aqueduct on the Llangollen Canal dates from the same year. While the rest of the country was honouring Nelson, canal enthusiasts in North Wales were quietly raising a glass to Telford whose legacy, one could argue, is the longer lasting.

On 26th November, 2005 a crowd in excess of two thousand braved a Welsh downpour to mark the aqueduct's 200th year with a sixteen cannon salute and the passage over the bridge of the restored Shropshire Union fly boat *Saturn*. Mr Telford even returned for the day to address the crowd, as quite possibly he had done two hundred years earlier; though there were some present who have begun to believe that he stole the limelight from William Jessop!

Perhaps we will never really ascertain where the real credit lies, perhaps it doesn't really matter. The one sure truth is that Pontcysyllte is the dramatic highlight of the UK's most popular canal, an icon which every canal boater will want to have crossed before they hang up their windlass. Naturally, I hope they will use this guide to get them there. This is its seventh edition and a quarter of a century has elapsed since we first crossed Pontcysyllte ourselves to research it for you. Which means that for one eighth of its existence Pontcysyllte Aqueduct has featured in a Pearson's Canal Companion and, what's more, there is no

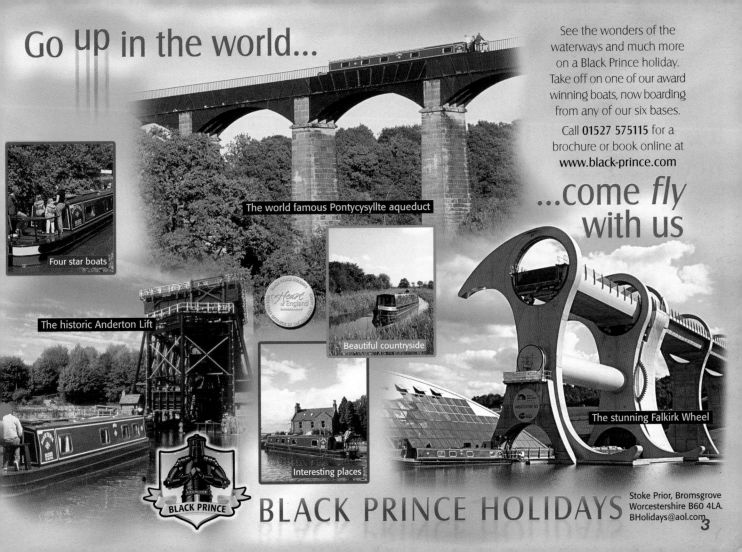

Go up in the world...

See the wonders of the waterways and much more on a Black Prince holiday. Take off on one of our award winning boats, now boarding from any of our six bases.

Call **01527 575115** for a brochure or book online at **www.black-prince.com**

...come *fly* with us

Four star boats

The world famous Pontycysyllte aqueduct

The historic Anderton Lift

Beautiful countryside

Interesting places

The stunning Falkirk Wheel

BLACK PRINCE

BLACK PRINCE HOLIDAYS

Stoke Prior, Bromsgrove Worcestershire B60 4LA. BHolidays@aol.com

3

UK-BOATING*holidays*

If you are looking for a boating holiday you need look no further

Hire direct from the leading narrowboat operators with all boats inspected and awarded star ratings by Visit Britain.

A fleet of over 180 boats for 2 to 12 people from 11 start bases throughout the UK so you can be sure of the widest choice.

Beginners are welcome

Visit our website or telephone for a free brochure pack.

08701 217 670

www.uk-boating.com

Countrywide
Cruisers

Luxury holidays afloat

At Countrywide, the fine reputation which we now enjoy has been established with a fleet of narrowboats of exceptional comfort and reliability, built and operated by a team with a wealth of experience.

We turn round a maximum of five boats on any one day with the result that we are able to devote considerable resources to the cleaning and servicing of each one. Rest assured that you will take over an immaculate boat in the peak of operating condition.

Countrywide Cruisers (Brewood) Ltd,
The Wharf, Brewood, Staffordshire ST19 9BG
T: +44 (0)1902 850166 F: +44 (0)1902 851662
E: info@countrywide-cruisers.com
W: www.countrywide-cruisers.com

5

Napton Narrowboats
for the best canal holidays
Shropshire Union and South
Oxford Canal bases
Tel: 01926 813644 for brochure
Try our King Size double beds on Elite Class boats!

www.BoatingInEngland.co.uk

The
SHROPSHIRE UNION
Canal

LADY LEE

H&L RICHARDSON

WORKSOP

Reg No 503432

1 SHROPSHIRE UNION CANAL

Autherley Junction 3mls/1lk/1hr

DESPITE the proximity of Wolverhampton, Autherley, like many canal junctions, is self-contained. It is not pretty in a conventional sense, being bordered by housing estates, sewage plants and public open spaces. In typically pithy fashion, the old boatmen called it 'Cut End', for the obvious reason that the Shropshire Union Canal began and, more pertinently, ended here. Once there was all the paraphernalia of a meeting of waterways: toll office, stables, workshops, employees cottages, and a dominant, sweeping roving bridge carrying the Staffs & Worcs towpath over the entrance to the Shropshire Union. A stop lock - just six inches deep - protected the two companies' precious water supplies. Much of this infrastructure survives, enjoying a new lease of life in the leisure age as a hire base and boatyard.

A massive sewage plant provides the canal with much of its water; suitably treated of course, or perhaps this explains the Shropshire Union's apparent impatience to get on with its journey to the north-west. Whatever the motivation, Autherley is soon forgotten as the canal crosses the boundary between the West Midlands and Staffordshire and leaves the housing estates of suburban

Wolverhampton behind. The land east of the canal was once occupied by an aerodrome, whilst the works by Bridge 4 was formerly an aircraft factory, turning out, amongst other designs, the 'Defiant' fighter plane.

An 'invisible' aqueduct carries the canal over the little River Penk before the waterway goes through a series of contortions which see it narrowing, then widening, then narrowing again before resuming its usual width beyond Bridge 6. Jonathan Morris, a former lock-keeper, theorised in his detailed towpath guide to the canal that the narrow sandstone cuttings were cost-cutting exercises, brought about by cash-flow difficulties as the canal was being built. The wider pool beyond Bridge 5 - known locally as 'The Hattons' or 'figure o'three' - he suggests, related to former clay workings done on site as it were. The M54 intrudes a moment of modern reality, but otherwise the landscape is peacefully rural, setting the scene for the forty mile journey to Nantwich through some unexpectedly remote countryside.

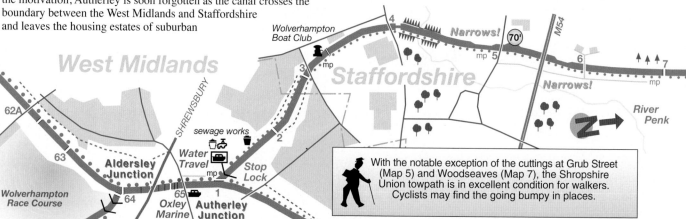

With the notable exception of the cuttings at Grub Street (Map 5) and Woodseaves (Map 7), the Shropshire Union towpath is in excellent condition for walkers. Cyclists may find the going bumpy in places.

THE Shropshire Union slices through the Staffordshire countryside in cuttings and upon embankments typical of the bold, 19th century designs of Thomas Telford, who engineered this route between Autherley and Nantwich, originally known as the Birmingham & Liverpool Junction Canal. Travelling northwards you rapidly become attuned to the unique atmosphere of this canal. Far from becoming monotonous, its purposeful, loping stride across the landscape is strangely exhilarating, perhaps due to the recurring contrast of shadowy cuttings and panorama providing embankments, known as 'rockings' and 'valleys' respectively to past generations of boatmen.

There are two notable structures either side of Brewood. To the south the distinctly ornate, balustraded Avenue Bridge (No 10) carries the carriageway to Chillington Hall. The advent of the canals heralded many similar attempts at ornamentation and disguise, where powerful landowners would only condescend to permit a waterway to cross their parklands if suitable steps were taken to adorn the otherwise purely functional architecture of the new trade route. In contrast, north of Brewood, the canal crosses the old Roman Road of Watling Street on a sturdy, yet elegant aqueduct of iron, brick and stone construction. Nearby Belvide Reservoir is one of the main sources of water supply for the Shropshire Union Canal, whilst Broom Hall, east of Bridge 16, was the home of William Carlos who hid King Charles II in the oak tree at nearby Boscobel after the Battle of Worcester in 1651.

Brewood

A lovely village, retaining an ancient air of calm. The natives call it 'Brood', and there really is a timelessness about it which seduces you into spending longer here than you might have planned. Winding lanes of gracious houses lead to the old market place where the distinctive vehicles of the Green Bus Company pause before rumbling off to Wolverhampton. Enhancing one corner of the square is 'Speedwell Castle', a Gothic fantasy erected in the 18th century on the winnings of a racehorse named Speedwell.

CONNOISSEUR TEA ROOMS - corner of the Square. All day licensed cafe/bar. Sunday carvery. Tel: 01902 851694.
ADMIRAL RODNEY - Dean Street. Tel: 01902 850583. Les Routiers recommended pub with good choice of food.
BRIDGE INN - Bridge 14. Much extended former boatmans pub. Burtonwood beers. Tel: 01902 850778.
SWAN HOTEL - Market Place. Tel: 01902 850330. CAMRA recommended.

Old fashioned shops where you can eavesdrop on local gossip: baker, butcher, chemist, newsagent with post office counter, SPAR (with cash machine) and branch of Lloyds TSB Bank. Calor gas from garage by Bridge 14. COOPERS foodstore is excellent, also the VILLAGE BAKERY for filled baps.
BUSES - Frequent Green Bus Co services (Mon-Sat) to/from Wolverhampton; some run through to/from Wheaton Aston and are thus useful for one-way towpath walks. Tel: 0870 608 2 608.

WHEATON ASTON Lock is strangely solitary - the only one in 25 miles of canal; a telling statistic of Telford's engineering. For about a mile the canal penetrates the deciduous heart of Lapley Wood, and there's another typical Shroppie cutting by Little Onn, but elsewhere the embankments offer wide views eastwards towards Cannock Chase.

How astonishingly remote and unpeopled the landscape seems. The West Midlands conurbation is less than a dozen miles to the south, yet moor for the night between Wheaton Aston and Little Onn, and you'll have only the occasional eerie hoot of a hunting owl, or the distant silent wash of headlights on a country lane, for company.

Abandoned wartime aerodromes inevitably have their ghosts, and in decay accumulate a patina of lore and legend, hard perhaps to equate with the often mundane use to which they were put after closure. Wheaton Aston was opened in 1941 and became one of the RAF's largest training units, operating a squadron of 'Oxfords'. There were at least two canal dramas. Once an American 'Thunderbolt' crash-landed in the waterway. Another well remembered wartime incident occurred at the lock when a narrowboat, carrying an unsheeted cargo of shining aluminium on a moonlit night, was attacked by a German aircraft which unleashed a bomb that exploded less than a hundred yards from the chamber. Swords into ploughshares: after the war the aerodrome became a pig farm!

Coach & Horses

Wheaton Aston

Spar
Hartley
Arms

stop
gate

*Lapley
Wood
Cutting*

70'

18

**Wheaton
Aston Lock**
7ft 0ins

19 mp 20

aqueducts

stop
gate

*former WWII
aerodrome*

Little Onn
Hall

20a

20b

20c
mp

21

22

2

17
mp

23 mp 24

4

"*Staffs Way" to/from Penkridge*

*By-road to
Penkridge*

Rye Hill Cutting

Wheaton Aston

Once purely a farming community, Wheaton Aston has been overwhelmed by modern housing. So it's certainly no picture postcard village, but at least it appears to be thriving, defying the trend towards rural decline, and a good shop makes it a useful port of call for the boater. Sadly, however, the French restaurant has closed down.

HARTLEY ARMS - canalside Bridge 19. Popular pub offering a good range of food. Tel: 01785 840232.
COACH & HORSES - village centre. Old fashioned Banks's local. Tel: 01785 841048.
Post office, newsagents, plus excellent SPAR opposite the church. It's open daily

7am-10pm and, along with all the other to be expected requisites, does a nice line in spit-roasted chickens and fresh-filled baguettes.Turner's canalside garage stocks Calor gas, diesel and boating accessories.
BUSES - Services to/from Brewood, Wolverhampton. Tel: 0870 608 2 608.

Wheaton Aston

Lord Talbot's Wharf

4 SHROPSHIRE UNION CANAL

THE buildings of two wharves remain intact at High Onn. One - now converted into a most desirable home - belonged to Cadbury's, the other to a local landowner, suggesting that there was once a degree of agricultural traffic on the canal. Deep shadowy sandstone cuttings, spanned by lichened grey stone bridges of simple balance and unaffected beauty, lead to the eighty-one unlined yards of Cowley Tunnel; the only one on the Shropshire Union. Once a dizzy jungle of trees darkened the approaches so much that you were never quite sure where the tunnel began and the cutting ended, but their roots caused instabilities in what was already a brittle rock strata and they were felled in 1985.

On a clear day the embankments north of Gnosall reveal that famous Shropshire landmark, The Wrekin, 15 miles to the south-west; a slumbering hunchback of a summit, 1335ft high. A. E. Housman celebrated it in *A Shropshire Lad,* and Salopians raise their glasses in a toast to: "All friends around the Wrekin".

Now in use as a public footpath, the dismantled railway line which crossed the canal at Gnosall once usefully connected Stafford with Shrewsbury until a certain doctor made his presence felt. Historically it was unusual in that it was actually built by the Shropshire Union Canal Company, apparently hedging their bets on the transport mode of the future. When, in 1846, they leased themselves to the London & North Western Railway, few shareholders would have backed the canal to outlast the railway as it has done.

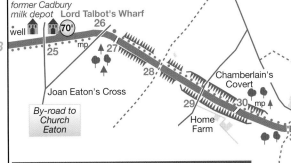

Gnosall Heath

This appendage of Gnosall (No-zull) grew up with the coming of the canal. Two pubs slaked the thirst of passing boatmen, a steam powered flour mill took advantage of the new transport mode, and a non-conformist chapel kept a sense of proportion amidst all the excitement. Nowadays the pubs pander to pleasure boaters and passing motorists and the flour mill and chapel have become private residences. Few boaters take the trouble to visit Gnosall itself, half a mile to the east, though it has a splendid church and further facilities.

THE BOAT - Bridge 34. Marston's/Banks's pub with attractive curved wall abutting the bridge. Food available and pleasant garden by the water's edge. Tel: 01785 822208.
THE NAVIGATION - Bridge 35. Nice garden with good children's playground. Tel: 01785 822327.

Fish & chips on A518 open daily (except Sundays), both sessions.
General store (with cash point) and butcher by Bridge 34. Another shop down the road and more shops in Gnosall.
BUSES - Arriva services to/from Stafford and Newport. Tel: 0870 608 2 608.

A MASK of tall trees disguises the immensity of Shelmore embankment. It was six years in the making and, in its way, was as glorious an engineering feat as any of Telford's more visibly imposing aqueducts. A vast army of navvies and horses was employed on it. Spoil from the big cuttings at nearby Gnosall and Grub Street was brought by wagon for its construction. To Telford's dismay the earthworks slipped time after time and, as the rest of the canal was finished, Shelmore stubbornly refused to hold. In poor health, Telford struggled to oversee its completion, conscious that the bank need not have been tackled at all, had Lord Anson of Norbury Park sanctioned the preferred course

through Shelmore Wood. Sadly, Norbury is no longer a junction, though the name lives on. How nice it would be to lock down the 'Seventeen Steps' of the Newport Branch and head across the marshy emptiness of Shropshire's Weald Moors to Shrewsbury. A feasibility study has recently put a cost of £86m on fully restoring the canal.

North of Norbury lies Grub Street cutting. For over a mile the canal is wrapped in a thick coat of vegetation, again, like Shelmore, hiding the sheer size of the eighty foot deep cutting, whose most unusual feature is the double-arched bridge which carries the A519 across the canal. The tiny telegraph pole is a survivor from the line which once marched beside the Shroppie for much of its length. Ironically, canals are again being used as lines of communication with the burying of optical fibres beneath selected lengths of towpath. It is to be hoped that this hi-tech activity meets with the approval of the black, monkey-like creature reputed to have haunted Bridge 39 ever since a boatman was killed here in the 19th century.

Walkers and cyclists alike will curse their way through Grub Street - have they never heard of duck-boards, let alone proper drainage?

Map labels:
4
mp
Shelmore Embankment
Course of Newport Branch
Norbury Junction
Junction Inn
Norbury
BW
70'
38
Norbury Wharf
mp
A519 from Newport
39
Grub Street Cutting
40
41
42
43
A519 to Eccleshall
70'
mp
The Anchor
mp
By-road to High Offley
6

Norbury Junction

An atmospheric canal community, and although the suffix is misleading nowadays, Norbury remains a busy canal centre where British Waterways have a maintenance yard. Some of the houses are still occupied by canal workers.

JUNCTION INN - canalside Bridge 38. Busy pub popular with boaters and motorists alike. Garden with children's play area. Bar and restaurant meals. Tel: 01785 284288. Gift shop in garden.

ANCHOR INN - canalside Bridge 42. Famously unspoilt boatman's pub serving Devizes-brewed Wadworth 6X from the jug. Gift shop to rear selling souvenirs and T-shirts. Tel: 01785 284569.
OLD WHARF TEA ROOMS - canalside Bridge 38.

Boatyard cafe and B&B - Tel: 01785 284292.
Boatyard shop: provisions, off licence, gifts. A truly useful facility for canal travellers between Gnosall and Market Drayton. Good choice of canal literature as well.

C ROSSING the border between Staffordshire and Shropshire, the canal continues to traverse an uncluttered countryside almost entirely given over to agriculture. It can come as a surprise to find so remote a landscape in the 'crowded' middle of England. One is tempted to categorise the area as 'lost' but for the obvious truth that it has never been 'found' in the first place.

Blithely we pleasure boaters sail across embankments and through cuttings with no more thought for their construction than if we were driving down the M6. But imagine the impact of Telford's brash new canal on the surrounding early nineteenth century landscape. Put yourself in the position of Sir Richard Whitworth's tenant farmer at Batchacre Park. Up until 1830 dawn rose across the open pasturelands throwing light through his east-facing windows. A year later his view of the rising sun was cut off forever by an embankment twice the height of the farmhouse. No wonder the landowners of this rural corner of Staffordshire had their misgivings, and the canal company paid dearly in compensation for the land they acquired.

West of the canal, there are good views of The Wrekin, with the Clee and Breidden hills prominent on the far horizon.

It comes as something of a surprise to encounter a confectionery factory in the midst of otherwise empty countryside. It was opened by Cadbury, the chocolate manufacturers, in 1911 as a centre for processing milk collected from the dairy farming hinterland of the Shropshire Union Canal. Canal transport was used exclusively to bring countless churns gathered from numerous wharves along the canal; from simple wooden stages at the foot of fields, to the sophistication of Cadbury's own plant at High Onn. Cadbury owned a distinctive fleet of narrowboats, being one of the first operators to experiment with motorised craft. Cocoa and sugar crumb were also brought by boat to Knighton and blended with milk to make raw chocolate, itself returned to Bournville, again by boat, to be transformed into the finished delicacy. The last boatman to trade to Knighton was Charlie Atkins senior; nicknamed 'Chocolate Charlie' for obvious reasons. He carried the final cargo from Knighton to Bournville in 1961. Since then all transport to and from the still busy works has been by road. Attempts to have the handsome Art Deco type canalside buildings demolished have, thus far at least, been staved off by a preservation order.

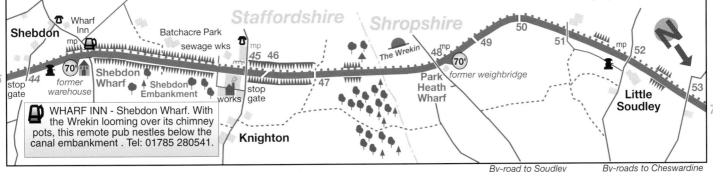

By-road from Forton

Wharf Inn

Shebdon

mp

Batchacre Park
sewage wks

Staffordshire   *Shropshire*

50

49   51

The Wrekin   48   52

5   44   70'   *former warehouse*   **Shebdon Wharf**   Shebdon Embankment   works   stop gate   47   mp   45   46   stop gate   70'   *former weighbridge*   Park Heath Wharf   mp   53   7

stop gate

WHARF INN - Shebdon Wharf. With the Wrekin looming over its chimney pots, this remote pub nestles below the canal embankment . Tel: 01785 280541.

Knighton

Little Soudley

By-road to Soudley   *By-roads to Cheswardine*

T HE Shroppie flirts with the county boundary, the towpath forming the demarcation so that, technically, the canal lies briefly in Staffordshire. The landscape, though, is impervious to the machinations of local government, remaining aloof and typically remote: a tall, dark, silent canal, this Shropshire Union.

WOODSEAVES is another prodigious cutting. The canal narrows and, in places, is cut through solid rock. These cuttings proved just as troublesome to Telford and his contractors as did the embankments. There were frequent avalanches during construction and, even today, brittle lumps of sandstone are inclined to dislodge themselves and tumble into the canal; one reason why a 2mph speed limit is imposed. Walkers will be grateful for the cool shade on hot days - cyclists might find the going tricky. A feature of Woodseaves is its pair of high bridges, spanning the canal like portals to the mysterious chasms of another world.

At TYRLEY a flight of five locks - the last to be faced southbound for seventeen miles - carries the canal down into, or up out of, Market Drayton. The lower chambers are located in a shadowy sandstone cutting across which branches intertwine to form a tunnel of trees. Damp and rarely touched by sunlight, all manner of mosses and ferns flourish in this conducive environment.

After dusk bats leave their tree bole roosts to hunt for insects, acrobatically twisting and turning over the luminous pounds between the locks. The well-surfaced towpath makes the flight popular with pedestrians but parking is restricted on the lane which crosses the canal by bridge 60. The provision of a sanitary station and rubbish point above the top lock satisfies the needs of boaters too.

TYRLEY WHARF was a point of discharge and collection for the local estate at Peatswood. The buildings date from 1837 and were erected in a graceful Tudor style by the local landowner. Nowadays, its commercial significance a thing of the dim and distant past, it would be difficult to imagine a more picturesque scene though it is sad that the craft shop and home-baking outlet, admirable enterprises of the 1980s, have both been and gone.

Summary of Facilities

Remote from any village, THE WHARF TAVERN by Bridge 55 is a popular port of call throughout the boating season and features a spacious canalside garden. Tel: 01630 661226. 10 minutes west of Tyrley Wharf you'll find THE FOUR ALLS - Tel: 01630 652995 which offers bar and restaurant meals and also accommodation.

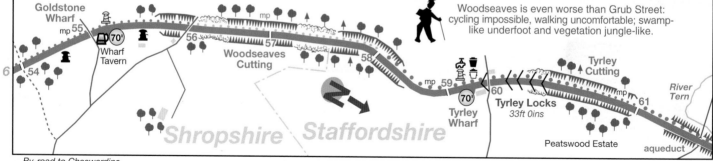

Woodseaves is even worse than Grub Street: cycling impossible, walking uncomfortable; swamp-like underfoot and vegetation jungle-like.

Goldstone Wharf

Wharf Tavern

Woodseaves Cutting

Tyrley Wharf

Tyrley Locks 33ft 0ins

Tyrley Cutting

Peatswood Estate

aqueduct

River Tern

Shropshire   Staffordshire

By-road from Market Drayton

By-road to Cheswardine

Tyrley Locks

MARKET DRAYTON was the largest, in fact the only, town encountered by the old Birmingham & Liverpool Junction Canal on its route from Autherley to Nantwich. Naturally, a sizeable wharf was provided for dealing with local cargoes; though the canal's monopoly on local trade lasted only thirty years before the railway reached the town. It is sometimes difficult, in these days of the ubiquitous juggernaut, to appreciate the importance of the canal wharf and the railway goods yard to the past prosperity of small towns like Drayton. They must have been the hub of local life, few businesses would have been able to carry out their trade without regular recourse to the wharfinger and the stationmaster. From the opening of the canal until the First World War no commodity, apart from local agricultural produce, could have arrived at Market Drayton, or been dispatched, without the involvement of these important gentlemen. On the canal a large basin and a sizeable warehouse and adjoining cornmill remind us of this lost significance.

Pleasant 48 hour moorings, bordered by school playing fields, stretch

south from Bridge 62 to the imposing aqueduct over the lane to Peatswood. Steps lead down to the road below, which crosses the little River Tern nearby and forms the most romantic, but not the most convenient, approach to the town centre.

By Bridge 65, H. Orwell & Son continue in business as coal merchants from their lugubrious red brick premises. Note the substantial stone abutments where the North Staffordshire Railway once crossed the canal. Another long lost railway accompanies the canal past Adderley.

BETTON CUTTING is not among 'The Shroppie's' most dramatic, but it is reputed to be haunted by a shrieking spectre, and working boatmen would avoid lingering here in the old days. Indeed, it could be said that this whole canal has something of a fey quality about it, a blurring of past and present which is liable to send shivers down susceptible spines.

The ADDERLEY flight is neat and tidy, although not the place it was when every chamber was bordered by flower beds and the grass manicured like a bowling green. A privet hedge beside the third lock down indicates the site of a demolished lock-keeper's cottage, one of many to have disappeared from the canal system over the years.

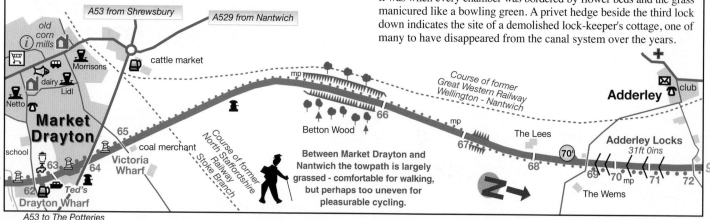

Market Drayton

The conspicuous Second World War pillbox guarding Bridge 62 is not, despite first impressions, still in situ as a deterrent to visitors. Self-styled as 'The Home of Gingerbread', Drayton is best visited on a Wednesday when the ancient market is in full swing and country folk gather to seek out a bargain and a gossip. This is the town's real heritage, along with its half-timbered houses which mostly date from the aftermath of a fire which swept through the place in 1651. Drayton's most famous son was Robert Clive, best remembered here for scaling the sturdy tower of St Mary's and for blackmailing local shopkeepers - ideal escapades in preparation for a career in diplomacy and military leadership. He established British rule in the Sub Continent and became known as 'Clive of India'. Betjeman and Piper's Shell Guide of 1951 recalls that the district was once terrorised by a murderous gang known as "The Bravoes of Market Drayton". On Saturday nights, as the pubs empty, it's easy to believe they are still at large. To the west of the town lie the large premises of Muller - "the UK's most loved dairy product brand" - whilst on the northern fringe is Drayton's Livestock Market, a flourishing centre for agricultural buying and selling.

THE TALBOT - adjacent Bridge 62. Tel: 01630 661226. A handsome, red brick Georgian inn just east of the canal. Accommodation available.

STAFFORD COURT HOTEL - Stafford Street. Tel: 01630 652646. Bar & restaurant food in small, but well-appointed town centre hotel.

DRAYTON HOUSE - Sherwood Crescent. Chinese take-away. Tel: 01630 658992.

THE BUTTERCROSS - town centre tea room: coffees, traditional hot food, teas & gifts.

It isn't easy for small market towns to compete these days, let alone small independent shops, but Market Drayton does its best and still bustles on a Wednesday, market day. WILLIAMS OF WEM is a fine delicatessen beside the Buttercross. Branches of all the main banks, a post office, launderette and Lidl, Morrisons, KwikSave, and Netto supermarkets will cater adequately to most boaters' requirements.

TOURIST INFORMATION - Cheshire Street. Tel: 01630 652139.

BUSES - X64 services approximately bi-hourly, daily to/from Stoke and Shrewsbury, with one bus operating to/from Audlem on market day - useful for one-way towpath walks. Tel: 0870 608 2 608.

TAXIS - First Call Taxis. Tel: 01630 653200.

FIFTEEN locks running through a cutting of larch and Scots pine take the canal across the Shropshire/Cheshire border. The locks are well-maintained and a pleasure to operate. Vegetables and fruit are often available from an honesty box by Lock 9. The barrel-roofed building by Lock 10 was used by stonemasons, blacksmiths and carpenters engaged in maintaining the flight. Towards the foot of the flight - known to old boatmen as the Audlem "Thick" - you pass Audlem Wharf, one of the prettiest ports of call on the Shropshire Union, with a former warehouse restored as a popular pub and the adjacent lofty mill converted into a superb craft shop.

North of the bottom lock, below which is a well preserved stable block used as a base by the Daystar Theatre Group, the canal, wide with concrete banking but deceptively shallow, bounds across the infant River Weaver on a high embankment. One of the crazier notions of the Ministry of War Transport during the Second World War was to make the Weaver navigable by 100 ton barges to this point, beyond which a lift would carry them up to the level of the Shropshire Union, upgraded sufficiently for them to travel as far south as Wolverhampton. Pleasure boaters can be thankful that this scheme never got off the drawing board and can moor at the foot of the Audlem flight in splendid isolation.

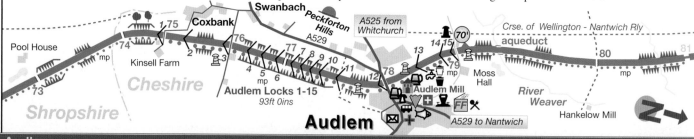

Audlem

"The sleepers sleep at Audlem" sang Flanders and Swann in *Slow Train*, their elegy for the Beeching cuts, and whilst they were referring to the village's station and its imminent closure, Audlem remains a sleepy place. Now that the trains have gone and the average motorist is hell bent on getting somewhere else as fast as he can, only the canal traveller is journeying at a pace to do justice to this lovely village, highpoints of which are the ancient buttermarket and parish church.

THE BRIDGE - canalside Bridge 78. Marstons, food. Tel: 01270 811267.

THE SHROPPIE FLY - canalside Lock 13. Nicely furnished warehouse conversion serving bar and restaurant meals. Tel: 01270 81772.
THE LORD COMBERMERE - The Square. Popular village local. Food, families welcome. Tel: 01270 811316.
THE PLAICE - Cheshire Street. Fish & chips.
OLD PRIESTS HOUSE - The Square. Coffees, teas and light lunches.
KEBAB & PIZZA HOUSE - Tel: 01270 812226.
BUSES - services to/from Nantwich and Whitchurch on Weekdays and (curiously) Crewe on Sundays. Tel: 0870 608 2 608.

Friendly shops cater for most needs and make shopping here a pleasure rather than a stressful chore. Many shops indulge in a lunchtime siesta though, and Wednesday is half-day. Ice cream, produced on the premises, is available from the old fashioned confectioners by the market cross. Cash machine at the Co-op. Audlem's outstanding establishment, however, is the AUDLEM MILL CANAL SHOP converted from the three-storey Kingbur Mill by John Stothert in 1976. Shopping and browsing here is, in the proprietor's own words: "Just as much a social event as a retail experience." And how!

AT Hack Green there are two isolated locks and the remnants of a stable, recalling the practice of frequent changing of horses on the 'fly' boats which travelled day and night with urgent, perishable cargoes. This is the Cheshire Plain and dairy farming has long been a vital part of the area's economy - though for how much longer one might wonder, given the precarious state of agriculture at the beginning of the 21st century. We tend to think of farming as an unchanging facet of the landscape, but the Friesian cattle synonymous with milk production would have seemed like interlopers to 19th century boatmen more used to indigenous British breeds like Ayrshires and Alderneys.

Unchanging landscape! Thank goodness this is comparatively true, for when we first explored this canal in the early Eighties we were blissfully unaware of Hack Green's nuclear bunker, a Second World War radar station secretly designated to play a role as a Regional Government Headquarters in the event of a nuclear war. Deemed redundant at the end of the Cold War, it has somewhat bizarrely become a tourist attraction:

fascinating stuff, but more than a little unnerving too.

Adroitly changing the subject, let us recall how trade survived on this canal until the 1960s; which must be some sort of testimony to the viability of canal carrying. Perhaps in the final analysis attitudes rather than economics prevailed. One of the most celebrated traffics on the Shroppie in latter years was Thomas Clayton's oil run from Stanlow on the banks of the Mersey to Langley Green, near Oldbury in the Black Country. The contract commenced in 1924 and the Clayton boats, with their characteristic decked holds, and river names, were a mainstay of trade on the canal for thirty years. Even post-war, a thousand boat-loads per annum were being despatched from Stanlow, some remaining horse-drawn until the early Fifties. But, in common with other canals, the Shropshire Union lost its final freights to the motor lorry; then, for many, with the disappearance of its working boats, something died on the Shroppie, some intangible component of canal heritage that no amount of preservation, nor hectic holiday trade, can ever compensate for.

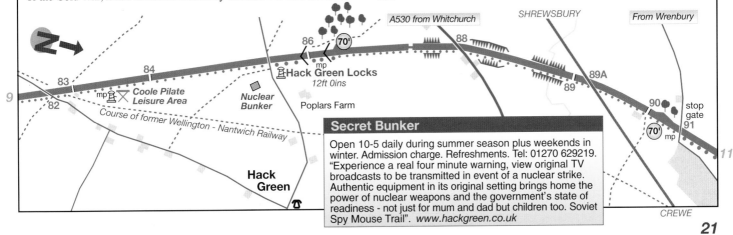

Secret Bunker

Open 10-5 daily during summer season plus weekends in winter. Admission charge. Refreshments. Tel: 01270 629219. "Experience a real four minute warning, view original TV broadcasts to be transmitted in event of a nuclear strike. Authentic equipment in its original setting brings home the power of nuclear weapons and the government's state of readiness - not just for mum and dad but children too. Soviet Spy Mouse Trail". *www.hackgreen.co.uk*

T HE character of the Shropshire Union Canal changes perceptibly at Nantwich: northwards lie the broad, winding waters of its earlier constituent, the Chester Canal; southwards the direct and narrow Birmingham & Liverpool Junction Canal. A broad embankment elevates the canal above the housing, back gardens and allotments which constitute the periphery of Nantwich. Ironically, these earthworks, together with a cast iron aqueduct over the Chester road, could have been avoided if the owners of Dorfold Hall had not objected to the passage of the canal across their land. The basin and former terminus of the Chester Canal, indicating the more expedient route to the south which Telford would have liked to have used, nowadays provides valuable mooring space, long term and short term, and there is a certain pleasure to be had from manoeuvring in and out of its narrow confines. Adjoining the basin are the premises of the Nantwich & Border Counties Yachting Club. Between Nantwich and Hurleston Junction (Map 12) the Chester Canal, dating from 1779, passes uneventfully through a landscape typical of the Cheshire Plain.

Nantwich

The octagonal tower of St Mary's church, glimpsed across freshly-built rooftops from the high canal embankment, tempts you to moor and get to know this picturesque and historic Cheshire town. Walking in from the basin, the aqueduct forms an appropriate portcullis, and the appeal of the town increases as the centre is reached. Few English towns are cleaner or better endowed with floral displays. In medieval times Nantwich was the chief salt producing town in the county. For a brief Victorian heyday it flourished as a spa town.

ODDFELLOWS ARMS - Welsh Row. Tel: 01270 624758. Likeable Burtonwood local less than 5 minutes from the canal aqueduct.
McCORMICK'S - Pepper Street. Tel: 01270 628451. Lively coffee house.
VINE INN - Hospital Street. Tel: 01270 624172. Hydes ales and a good menu.
CURSHAWS - Welsh Row. Tel: 01270 623020. Stylish modern eaterie on way into town.
BUSES - Tel: 0870 608 2 608.
TRAINS - services to/from Crewe and Shrewsbury. Tel: 08457 484950.

More affluent than Whitchurch or Market Drayton, Nantwich's antique shops and boutiques emphasise its position at the centre of a well-heeled hinterland. But it is perhaps the food sellers that are most satisfying: butchers like CLEWLOWS, bakers like CHATWINS and fishmongers like SEA BREEZES all of whom have branches in Pepper Street. On Hospital Street make a bee line for WELCH, a butchers, grocers, delicatessen and coffee merchant. Across the street, there's a good dealer in classical, jazz and world music CDs, whilst on Pillory Street there's a fine wine merchant. A market is held on Thursdays and Saturdays, whilst Wednesday is half day closing. Laundry facilities are available at the canal basin.
(i) TOURIST INFORMATION - Church Walk. Tel: 01270 610983.
NANTWICH MUSEUM - Well presented displays of local history. Free admission. Tel: 01270 827104.

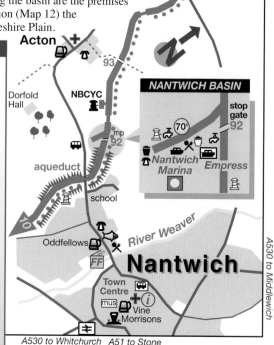

HURLESTON and Barbridge are the 'Clapham Junctions' of the inland waterways. During the cruising season the section between them is often frenetic with boats converging and diverging to and from all points of the canal compass.

Fortunately, the old Chester Canal was built to barge dimensions and there is plenty of room to manoeuvre. The Cheshire Plain's recurring image of spacious pastures grazed by Friesian cattle continues unabated.

Remote and frequently windswept, the Middlewich Branch of the Shropshire Union cuts across the grain of the landscape on a series of high embankments. It can be a busy length of canal for, as well as funnelling boats to and from the Llangollen Canal, it is also an integral component of the popular Four Counties Ring. There are four locks on the Middlewich; deep and heavy gated, they can become bottlenecks at the beginning and end of the week in high summer. Situated just below Cholmondeston Lock, Venetian Marine, one of the largest 'marina villages' on the canal system, adds to the hustle and bustle.

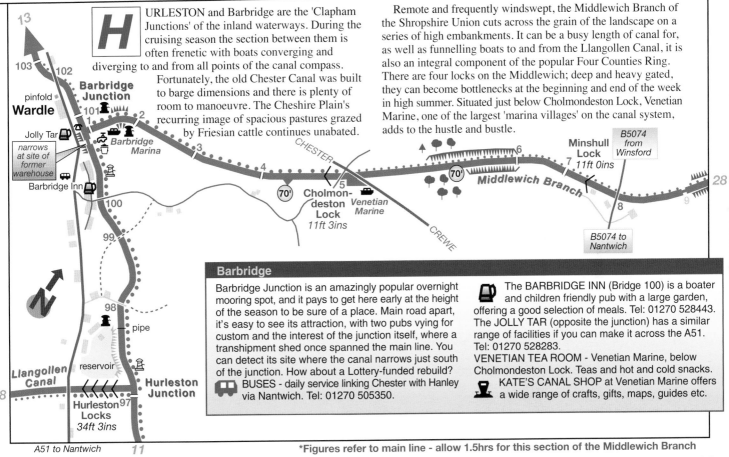

Barbridge

Barbridge Junction is an amazingly popular overnight mooring spot, and it pays to get here early at the height of the season to be sure of a place. Main road apart, it's easy to see its attraction, with two pubs vying for custom and the interest of the junction itself, where a transhipment shed once spanned the main line. You can detect its site where the canal narrows just south of the junction. How about a Lottery-funded rebuild?

🚌 BUSES - daily service linking Chester with Hanley via Nantwich. Tel: 01270 505350.

The BARBRIDGE INN (Bridge 100) is a boater and children friendly pub with a large garden, offering a good selection of meals. Tel: 01270 528443. The JOLLY TAR (opposite the junction) has a similar range of facilities if you can make it across the A51. Tel: 01270 528283.

VENETIAN TEA ROOM - Venetian Marine, below Cholmondeston Lock. Teas and hot and cold snacks.

KATE'S CANAL SHOP at Venetian Marine offers a wide range of crafts, gifts, maps, guides etc.

*Figures refer to main line - allow 1.5hrs for this section of the Middlewich Branch

Tilstone Bank

THIS is an intoxicating length of waterway, full of contrasts in landscape: the wooded defile at Tilstone Bank; the glorious line of close-cropped hills running north of the two Beeston locks; and most dramatic of all for travellers heading northwards, the first detailed glimpses of Beeston Castle, over five hundred feet high on its lonely outcrop. Through all this the little River Gowy chuckles to its Mersey outfall, draining the rolling farmland. But, scintillating scenery apart, it bears remembering that the old Chester Canal had a living to earn, and throughout this section there are well preserved examples of former commerce, notably the former transhipment wharf between canal and railway at Calveley, now under the aegis of British Waterways as a 'Service Station', offering showers and pumpout in addition to the usual boating facilities of water, rubbish and Elsan disposal.

Bunbury is a fascinating canal environment. The widebeam staircase locks make an obvious centrepiece. Alongside them is a fine stable block, recalling the practice of exchanging fresh horses for tired ones on the fast 'fly boats' which covered the 80 miles between the Mersey ports and the Black Country factories in just over 24 hours. These premises are now occupied by Anglo Welsh, their offices and shop being accommodated in an adjacent warehouse still displaying the faded legend 'Shropshire Union Railway & Canal Co' on its north facing gable end.

Tilstone Lock lies in a gorgeous setting. Beside it a mill stands astride the Gowy, dating from 1838 and tenderly restored for residential use. A curious circular building overlooks the head of the lock chamber. There are others at Beeston and Tarvin locks and they were once used by lengthsmen to store maintenance equipment. Beneath a sweeping ridge reminiscent of the South Downs stand the two Beeston locks; the upper built conventionally of stone, the lower unusually of iron plates - Telford's way of dealing with ground instability at this point; it is not advisable to attempt fitting two narrow boats side by side in this lock.

Summary of Facilities

At Calveley there's a bar/grill called THE GOLDMINE - Tel: 01829 262550. The garage by shop 103A boasts a shop and cash machine. BUNBURY MILL, a restored water mill beside the Gowy, a few hundred yards south-west of Bridge 105, is open to the public on Sunday and Bank Holiday afternoons between April and September. Tel: 01829 261422. The BEESTON CASTLE HOTEL is a popular pub/restaurant, especially on Wednesdays and Fridays when the cattle market is in full swing. LOCK GATE CAFE by Bridge 107 is open daily for breakfasts, lunches and teas. Anglo Welsh also have a cafe at their Bunbury boatyard.

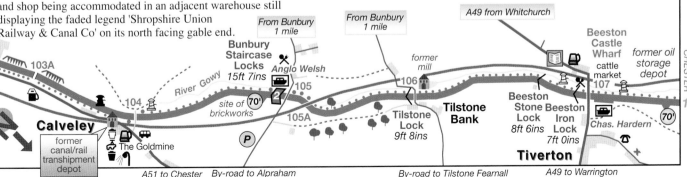

BEESTON Castle dominates the landscape, like a visitor from another planet, an upturned plum pudding of an outcrop, a geological afterthought commandeered by Medieval man for a fortress. Behind it the Peckforton Hills ride the horizon like surfers on an Atlantic beach. This is good hiking country. The Sandstone Trail, a 30 mile footpath across Cheshire's backbone from Overton to Whitchurch, crosses the canal at Wharton's Lock and may be conveniently linked with the towpath and other public footpaths to form a number of circular walks.

Bates Mill survives as an enviable private residence. A country road swoops down to cross the millstream and an adjacent expanse of water is the haunt of wildfowl. Nearby, the canal is carried over the Gowy on an embankment framed with conifers. Trains thread their way through the fields in the middle distance, but otherwise the world seems undisturbed. In the long pound between Wharton's and Christleton locks the boater has plenty of time for peaceful reflection and communion with nature.

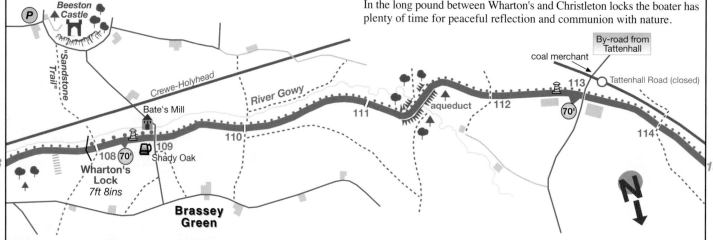

Beeston Castle

SHADY OAK - canalside Bridge 109. Tel: 01829 733159. Long established canalside pub with garden offering grandstand views of Beeston Castle. Take-aways are on offer, together with early morning breakfasts and bike hire.

i BEESTON CASTLE lies one mile south of Wharton's Lock along the Sandstone Trail. Open daily, 10am-6pm summer, 10am-4pm winter. Admission charge. Tel: 01829 260464. Captured at least three times during its turbulent history, by Simon de Montfort in his revolt against Henry III, and by both the Roundheads and Cavaliers during the Civil War, this 13th century fortress commands a wonderful panorama from its upper keep, the canal being discernible all the way to Egg Bridge.

ALTHOUGH the countryside is conspicuously flat, the Peckforton Hills to the south and Delamere Forest to the north-east give your gaze something to linger over; whilst, if the elements have blessed you with a clear day, the brooding summits of Celtic Wales are to be discerned on the western rim of the world.

Long lines of moored craft make the responsible boater's progress irritatingly slow in the vicinity of Hargrave. Smart boats, sad boats, new boats, neglected boats echo their absent owners' character and commitment; even some of the names mock at aspirations unachieved.

Probably the very earliest hire cruisers on the canal system were available from a boatyard at Christleton which began hiring to intrepid holidaymakers way back in 1935. In those days you could hire a small cruiser for £4 a week, though you also had to fork out ten shillings in tolls to the LMS Railway who owned the canal prior to Nationalisation in 1947.

In the late Twenties, a Chester man, T. W. Cubbon, wrote a charming account (*Only a Little Cockboat*) of a voyage, in a canvas covered open boat powered by a petrol engine, from Chester along the Shropshire Union and Staffs & Worcs canals to the rivers Severn and Avon. In the book he relates his first night on the canal at Egg Bridge moored abreast a widebeam barge, but being forced to move on in the small hours of the morning because rats from the barge had boarded his boat! The barges and the rats may have gone, but signs of former commerce remain at Egg Bridge and Christleton in the form of handsome canalside mills. At Christleton the canal commences its descent to Chester and the surface of the towpath improves, being conspicuously well-maintained all the way from here to Ellesmere Port.

Egg Bridge & Christleton

Egg Bridge offers useful facilities east of Bridge 119. They include a ONE STOP convenience store (with cash machine), a deli/sandwich bar, and PIZZA GUY (Tel: 01244 336006) which does breakfasts, baguettes, pizzas, kebabs and fish & chips, so you won't go hungry here.

Between bridges 120 and 121 the CHESHIRE CAT (Tel: 01244 332200) is one of those "Inn Keeping with Tradition" restaurant/pubs which can usually be relied upon to provide a good meal in comfortable surroundings. There are good moorings hereabouts too, whilst buses run into Chester from Bridge 122 - Tel: 01244 602666.

THE canal traveller's approach to the centre of Chester is overtly suburban and industrial, characteristics which belie the grace and romance of the city within its walls. Frankly, you could be forgiven for thinking that a Blackburn or a Burnley lay immediately ahead and it is with some relief that the centre is reached and the Chester of the tourist propaganda manifests itself. Yet even workaday Chester has its highlights: the dour Victorian waterworks below Chemistry Lock, then the high lead shot tower and gaunt warehouses which overlook the canal as it passes through an area of the city once vital to the coffers of the Shropshire Union. Widebeam barges known as Mersey 'flats' traded down from Ellesmere Port to Chester and, less often, southwards to Barbridge and Nantwich.

West of the centre lies Tower Wharf and the short Dee Branch linking the canal with the river. The canalscape here is full of interest: Telford's warehouse with its arched loading bay; an elegant canopied drydock; a large boatbuilding yard where the Shropshire Union carrying fleet was once built and maintained; and the rare fascination of two adjacent canal levels. The former North Basin - thoughtlessly infilled in the Fifties - has recently been re-dug and re-watered as part of a redevelopment scheme. A plaque on Bridge 126 commemorates L. T. C. Rolt's championing of the canals.

But it is the canal's juxtaposition with Chester's great red medieval wall which is its most memorable gesture and image. The round tower from which King Charles I saw his Cavaliers beaten looms out over the water so dramatically that the canal resembles a defensive moat, which is exactly what it once was, and the canal builders took good advantage of this defensive channel. Not so easy was the construction of the gargantuan Northgate staircase locks which had to be hewn out of solid rock.

The Chester Canal predated the Wirral Line by a matter of twenty years or so and, originally, the link with the River Dee continued direct from the foot of Northgate Locks, which at that time consisted of five chambers. The existing layout dates from the advent of the route from Ellesmere Port and the branch down to the Dee describes a dogleg course through three locks to meet the tidal river; a waterway not for novices! - Tel: 01244 324324.

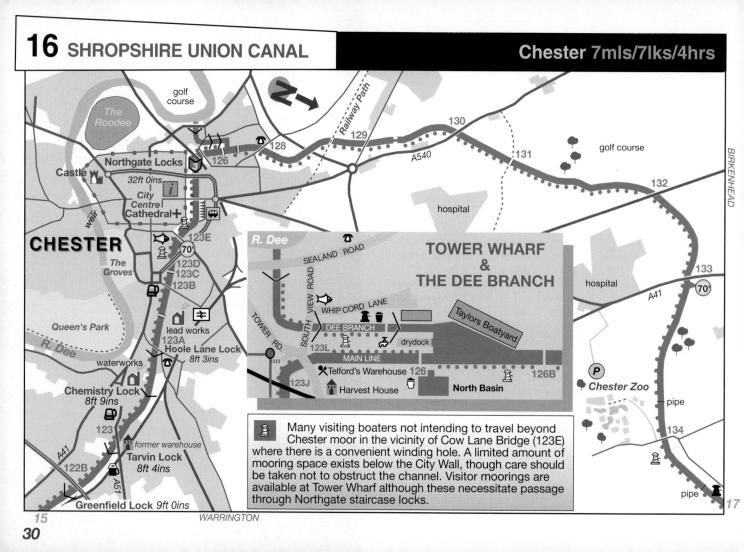

golf course

The Roodee

Railway Path

130

129

128

126

A540

131

golf course

132

Northgate Locks

Castle

32ft 0ins

City Centre

Cathedral

CHESTER

hospital

BIRKENHEAD

The Groves

123E

70'

123D
123C
123B

R. Dee

SEALAND ROAD

SOUTH VIEW ROAD

TOWER RD.

TOWER WHARF & THE DEE BRANCH

hospital

133

A41

70'

Queen's Park

R. Dee

WHIP CORD LANE

DEE BRANCH

Taylors Boatyard

drydock

123A

lead works

Hoole Lane Lock
8ft 3ins

123J

123

MAIN LINE

Telford's Warehouse

126

Harvest House

North Basin

126B

P

Chester Zoo

pipe

134

waterworks

Chemistry Lock
8ft 9ins

123

former warehouse

Tarvin Lock
8ft 4ins

122B

A41

A51

Greenfield Lock *9ft 0ins*

pipe

17

Many visiting boaters not intending to travel beyond Chester moor in the vicinity of Cow Lane Bridge (123E) where there is a convenient winding hole. A limited amount of mooring space exists below the City Wall, though care should be taken not to obstruct the channel. Visitor moorings are available at Tower Wharf although these necessitate passage through Northgate staircase locks.

15

WARRINGTON

Chester

On Sunday mornings, Chester breathes like a sleeping child and footsteps echo your progress around the city wall, the perfect introduction to this lovely city. At most other times, though, shoppers and tourists transform Chester into a frenetic, free-for-all from which you are apt to go scurrying back to your boat for refuge. But in all of Britain's inland waterways, only York can vie with Chester when it comes to antiquity, and the city wall, which kept enemies at bay down the centuries, now keeps 20th century reality in its place. Once through the ancient gateways you are wrapped in a Medieval time warp which makes Chester the most agreeable of places to saunter in and absorb the atmosphere.

It was the Romans who founded the city, seeing it as a likely place to build a port and keep a weather eye on the troublesome Marches; they called it Deva. In the Dark Ages the Anglo Saxons undid much of their predecessors' civilisation, but by the Middle Ages Chester was flourishing again and a 12th century writer noted ships from Aquitaine, Germany and Spain at berth in the shadow of the city wall. Chester's celebrated 'Rows' are thought to have had their origins during this period. These covered galleries above street level are quite unique, and elevate window-shopping into a pleasurable experience for all.

During the Civil War the city supported King Charles, but it did him little good for it was from the walls of Chester that he saw his army defeated on Rowton Heath. Victorian Chester grew up outside the city wall, beyond the canal and out towards the railway. What the Victorians did inside the wall is best forgotten by those romantics who like to think that all that black and white half timbering is original. Today, though, Chester knows that it pays to look old. The city is on every tourist's 'must see' list and people flock here from all over the world - from Europe, America, Japan and Australia - to shop in the 'Rows', to picnic by the Dee, to walk the walls and to find a sense of peace in the dignified Cathedral. Those who make their way here by canal are the really lucky ones, for they stand to gain the most of all.

MEDITERRANEAN RESTAURANT. Rufus Court. Tel: 01244 320004. Charming staff serve Mediterranean food in an authentic atmosphere. BOLLICINI - Rufus Court, Northgate. Tel: 01244 329932. Stylish restaurant bar. RISTORANTE SERGIO - St Werburgh St. Tel: 01244 314663. Italian close to the Cathedral.
TELFORD'S WAREHOUSE - Tower Wharf. Tel: 01244 390090. Eat and drink in Telford's handsome canal warehouse - what would the great man make of it? Weetwood beers from Tarporley and good choice of food.

OLD HARKER ARMS - Bridge 123B. Tel: 01244 344525. Warehouse conversion.
MILL HOTEL - by Bridge 123C. Tel: 01244 350035. Good food and a wide choice of real ale.
UNION VAULTS - Egerton Street (by Bridge 123 C). Back street local offering Wrexham brewed Plassey ales. Tel: 01244 322170.
THE SLOW BOAT - Bridge 123E. Tel: 01244 317873. Chinese restaurant overlooking the canal.
BOULEVARD DE LA BASTILLE - Bridge Street. Tel: 01244 348708. Cafe & piano bar.

One of the best shopping centres in Britain. THE ROWS contain some of the most up-market shops in the city within their fascinating galleries, whilst ST MICHAEL'S ARCADE is a Victorian arcade of soaring iron and glass reached off Bridge Street Row. THE FORUM is an indoor market open daily (except Sunday), where stalls specialise in fresh Cheshire produce, crafts and antiques. Really good cheese shop on Northgate.

TOURIST INFORMATION CENTRE - Town Hall, Northgate. Open daily. Tel: 01244 402385.
CHESTER CATHEDRAL - One of England's ecclesiastical masterpieces.
DEWA ROMAN EXPERIENCE - Pierpoint Lane. Tel: 01244 343407.
FAMILY HISTORY CENTRE - Bridge Street Row. Admission charge, open daily. Tel: 01244 402110.
GROSVENOR MUSEUM - Grosvenor Street. Museum of local history. Admission free, open daily. Tel: 01244 402008.
SIGHTSEEING WALKS - Accompanied walks depart daily from the TIC.
CITY SIGHTSEEING - open top bus tours. Tel: 01244 347457.
DEE BOAT TRIPS - From the boating station on The Groves aboard Bithells launches. Tel: 01244 325394.
CHESTER ZOO - One of Europe's finest zoos. Admission charge, open daily. Best reached from the canal via Bridge 134. Tel: 01244 380280.
BUSES - bus station on George Street off Northgate. Tel: 01244 602666.
TRAINS - railway station on City Road, reached from Bridge 123B. Regular services to Ellesmere Port for the Boat Museum. Tel: 08457 484950. Free bus link to city centre for rail ticket holders.

C OMPARATIVELY few boaters reaching Chester from the south elect to continue along the Shropshire Union main line to its historic terminus on the banks of the River Mersey at Ellesmere Port. Beguiled by Chester's magnificence they languish in its spell, prisoners of the misconception that nothing worthy of their attention lies beyond Tower Wharf. In fact exploring the northern end of the Shropshire Union and stopping short at Chester is akin to not listening to the end of Beethoven's 5th Symphony, or omitting the cheese board at the Savoy.

Travelling northwards, urban Chester is soon left behind and one enters seemingly remote pastureland of no great beauty, but where peace prevails. More linear moorings slow the boater, but such delays can be redeemed as you near Ellesmere Port where a good depth of water enables the throttle to be exercised without fear of making a wash.

Dating from 1795, the canal between Chester and Ellesmere Port was part of the grandiose Ellesmere Canal scheme to link the Mersey with the Severn. Known as the Wirral line, it quickly attracted traffic; not only freight but passengers too, for a horse-drawn packet service connected Chester with Ellesmere Port where travellers could change to another boat to reach Liverpool. The passenger business flourished until the coming of the Railway Age, freight well into it. Indeed, narrowboats continued to trade from Ellesmere Port with oil for the Midlands until the mid 1950s. One of the most famous of these craft, *Gifford*, may be seen at the Boat Museum. Now, of course, the railway has declined also; hard to believe that boat trains once raced this way from London to connect with Atlantic liners on the Mersey. Today's more mundane transport makes an appearance at Stoak in

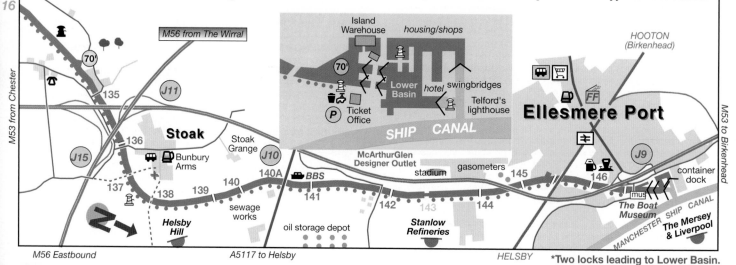

the shape of two motorways.

Northwards from Stoak, the gleaming refineries of Stanlow define themselves on the horizon, indicating that Ellesmere Port is near at hand. No-one would pretend, even in a guidebook, that the approach to the town is pretty, but anticipation outweighs purely aesthetic considerations, and there's a rising sense of excitement in anticipating your first sight of the Mersey.

A limited amount of mooring space is usually available between the motorway bridge and the museum entrance, for boaters intending to stay just a short time in the vicinity. Preferable though, in our opinion, are the spacious moorings in the lower basin reached through the locks. Here you can lie beside some of the Boat Museum's larger exhibits, such as the preserved ICI 'Brunner' barge *Cuddington* or the Clyde 'Puffer' *Basuto*.

Ellesmere Port, the 'port' of the Ellesmere Canal, dates from the last decade of the 18th century. The Wirral Line of the Ellesmere Canal met the Mersey here at what had, until then, been simply the small village of Netherpool. The opening of the Birmingham & Liverpool Junction Canal and later the Manchester Ship Canal turned these docks into a transhipment complex of almost unique significance. Happily, surviving neglect typical of the 1960s, much of the infrastructure was saved and incorporated into The Boat Museum, the country's premier collection of preserved inland waterway craft. One can't help but mourn, however, the loss through fire damage in 1970 of Telford's superb 'Winged Warehouses', three blocks of four storey structures which spanned part of the lower basin. Aerial photographs and diagrams exhibited in the museum illustrate the extent of the port in its heyday and emphasise the debt of gratitude owed to the small band of enthusiasts who began the collection of preserved craft which forms the basis of the museum.

Stoak

Largely uncompromised rural community despite presence of motorways on its doorstep. The BUNBURY ARMS (Tel: 01244 301665) is a well-appointed country pub offering a good choice of food. Moor in the vicinity of Bridge 138 and walk in past the church. Mon-Sat bus service to/from Chester & EP.

Ellesmere Port

In spite of new initiatives, Ellesmere Port remains a town with the sea in its blood if not on its doorstep. Snatches of conversation overheard in shops and pubs pertain to ships and seafarers and there's a salty, effervescent tang to the place which makes you long to weigh anchor and take to the briny. Regrettably, one senses that the emphasis has moved away from the seaward side of the town, its stevedoring and wharfingering, and the walk in, past tattoo parlours and pawn shops is a dispiriting glimpse of present-day priorities.

McDonalds, KFC and a Wetherspoons (named - what else - The Thomas Telford) on Whitby Road in the town centre.

Ten minutes walk through a seedy underpass takes you to the town centre where most chain stores are located in a 'standard' precinct; there's an indoor retail market too. CHESHIRE OAKS (McARTHURGLEN) Designer outlet centre accesible from Bridge 140A.

THE BOAT MUSEUM - Dockyard Road, Ellesmere Port, Cheshire L65 4EF. Open daily Apr-Oct, closed Thursdays and Fridays Nov-Mar. Admission charge. Britain's most extensive collection of preserved inland waterway craft; display areas in many of the former warehouses; boat trips, cafeteria and souvenir shop. Tel: 0151 355 5017. www.boatmuseum.org.uk

BUSES - services to Chester, Birkenhead etc from town centre bus station. Tel: 01244 602666.

TRAINS - services to Hooton for Liverpool and Chester. Tel: 08457 484950.

The LLANGOLLEN Canal

THROUGHOUT the summer, narrowboats glide through the broad emerald pastures of the Cheshire Plain, as measuredly as the high cumulus clouds in the wide Cheshire skies above. At Hurleston, a good proportion of them leave the main line of the old Shropshire Union, climb the four locks beside the reservoir embankment, and set off on the voyage to Wales. In terms of popularity 'The Llangollen' is the Blackpool of the canal system, but it has none of that seaside resort's vulgarity, owing its heavy holiday traffic to the enduring charm of its scenery and the vivid drama of its destination.

Hurleston locks raise the canal 34 feet. The reservoir stores water that has flowed down the canal from the River Dee at Horseshoe Falls above Llangollen itself, before it is treated and piped to the kitchen sinks of Crewe. Thank your lucky stars for this water; without it the LMS railway would have closed the canal during the Second World War, because trade had long since ceased. In fact, technically the canal was 'abandoned' and it was only its use as a water channel that saved it from the dereliction suffered by other LMS owned canals under the infamous Act of 1944.

Slowly, a new traffic of pleasure boats began using the canal, and under the 1968 Transport Act the Llangollen Canal (as the section of the old Ellesmere Canal between Hurleston and Llangollen had become known) was classified a 'cruiseway', its position as one of the premier canal holiday routes assured for posterity.

Between Hurleston and Wrenbury the waterway runs, surprisingly, on a North-South axis; subconsciously one expects to be travelling East-West. From Bridge 3 a footpath leads enticingly across the fields to Park Farm where the Sadlers make Snugburys Jersey Ice Cream - Tel: 01270 624830.

The locks at Swanley and Baddiley (Map 19) can become congested at busy times, like Friday afternoons when the exodus from Wales is at its height. Patience, patience!

The flow of water down the Llangollen Canal increases the running of the by-washes, causing a gush of water to run across the canal at the foot of locks. To compensate, steer slightly into the overflow. Going downhill, avoid being drawn over to the cill of the by-weir.

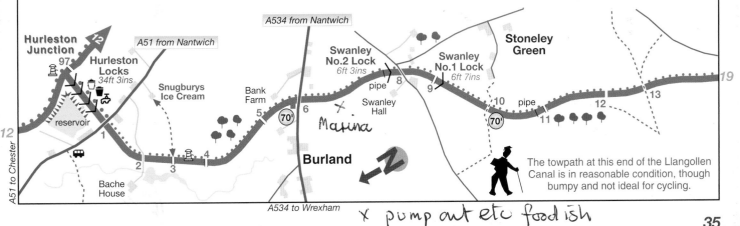

35

WRENBURY is one of the most picturesque ports of call at the English end of the Llangollen Canal. Bridge 20, rebuilt in timber and electrified (operated with a BW key), is equipped with less than discreet traffic lights but it would take more than these to spoil the attractive scene presented by the canal wharf and its old mills, now used as a pub and boatyard. The older of the two buildings dates back to the opening of the canal, though its site was used for a mill as early as the 16th century, power coming from the adjoining waters of the Weaver. On the opposite bank, the more modern mill appears to be of this century, being constructed in a handsome combination of corrugated iron and mellow brick. The former miller, Arthur Sumner, once operated a small fleet of narrowboats, but nowadays the mill serves as a hire fleet base and also houses a well stocked canal craft shop. Appropriately, some of Mr Sumner's descendants are now hosts at the "Dusty Miller".

Either side of Wrenbury, the Llangollen Canal wends its way through peaceful countryside of considerable charm. Inexperienced boaters sometimes tend to hurry along this section of the canal, anxious to reach the glories of Pontcysyllte and the Vale of Llangollen; a mistake in our view, like gulping down the hors d'oeuvres because you can't wait to get to the main course.

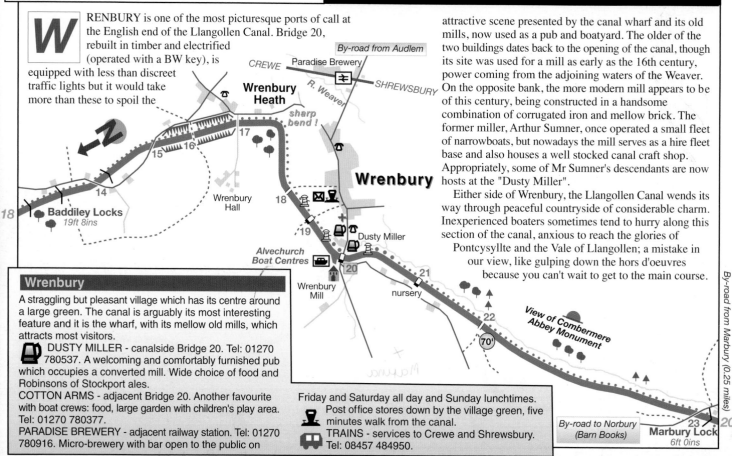

Wrenbury

A straggling but pleasant village which has its centre around a large green. The canal is arguably its most interesting feature and it is the wharf, with its mellow old mills, which attracts most visitors.

DUSTY MILLER - canalside Bridge 20. Tel: 01270 780537. A welcoming and comfortably furnished pub which occupies a converted mill. Wide choice of food and Robinsons of Stockport ales.

COTTON ARMS - adjacent Bridge 20. Another favourite with boat crews: food, large garden with children's play area. Tel: 01270 780377.

PARADISE BREWERY - adjacent railway station. Tel: 01270 780916. Micro-brewery with bar open to the public on Friday and Saturday all day and Sunday lunchtimes.

Post office stores down by the village green, five minutes walk from the canal.

TRAINS - services to Crewe and Shrewsbury. Tel: 08457 484950.

G RINDLEY BROOK is the focal point of this part of the Llangollen Canal. Here are six locks in close proximity, three of them forming a substantial 'staircase' overlooked by a splendid round-bayed lock-keeper's house typical of Telford's architectural style. In fact, the interest at Grindley Brook starts below the bottom lock where a fine skew bridge of blue engineering bricks still carries the trackbed of the old Chester to Whitchurch railway over the canal. A trio of single chambers precedes the staircase, the bottom of which is spanned by the Chester road, and bordered by old mill buildings.

The activity at Grindley Brook on a Bank Holiday weekend or busy summer's day, when between 60-100 boats may pass through the locks, provides wonderful entertainment for the spectator. The staircase locks, in particular, cause considerable congestion (especially on Thursdays) with delays of up to three hours often the result, and people react to the hold ups in different ways: some with frustration, some with patient resignation. The secret, of course, is to remember that you're on holiday and supposed to be enjoying yourself! The westbound boater, having climbed some forty feet through the six locks, does at least have twenty lock free miles to look forward to.

North of Grindley Brook the canal forms the county boundary between Cheshire and Shropshire for a short distance. The 'Sandstone Trail' swells the ranks of towpath walkers on this section. Reeds form a soothing curtain between the path and the water. South of Grindley Brook the canal makes as if to call at the old Shropshire market town of Whitchurch, but then seems to think better of it. A short branch terminated in the centre of town but was abandoned in 1944 and was subsequently, to the town's

Map labels:

Joyce's Clock Wks.

Tesco

former canal wharf

dairy

park

Whitchurch

proposed site of inclined plane

course of LNWR Chester - Whitchurch

Course of Whitchurch Arm

B5395

A49

A41

Danson's Farm

Viking

31

30A   31A   32

30

A41 to Newport / A525 to Newcastle-under-Lyme

A525 to Wrexham

21

Swan

Big Mere

Marbury

19

24

View of Peckforton Hills

Cheshire

Shropshire

Hinton Hall

Povey's Lock
6ft 7ins

Land of Canaan

Sandstone Trail

26

Grindley Brook Locks
38ft 11ins

former mill

Telford lock-keepers cottage
Lockside Stores

29

3

70'

28

Grindley Brook
Horse & Jockey

27

25

Quoisley Lock
6ft 0ins

Blind Bend!

Willey Moor Lock
6ft 0ins

Sandstone Trail

A49 to Warrington

A41 to Chester

regret, filled in. In 1993, however, a start was made in reclaiming the arm by restoring the first few hundred yards of it to provide moorings for visitors to the town. The next stage involves the construction of an inclined plane to detour around the original course of the canal which has been built over. Space has been left for this exciting development by the builders of two new housing estates. Meanwhile, you can follow the well-surfaced 'Sandstone Trail' into the town, and discover the former wharf, still apparent at the far end of Jubilee Park. In the good old days a weekly cargo of cheese left Whitchurch wharf bound for Manchester in a boat sheeted up with white canvas to deflect the sun's rays.

Whitchurch

Cheese and clocks are Whitchurch's gifts to civilisation. Blue Cheshire cheese is characterised by a marbled effect and is one of the great, tangy blue cheeses in the world. Joyce's, whose handsome premises stand on Station Road, have been manufacturing clocks for eight generations. The tower clock of the prominent St Alkmund's Parish Church is their work and dates from 1849. Whitchurch clocks have been exported all over the world and are to be found on many railway stations and other public buildings. In earlier days, when rail transport was paramount, completed clocks were carefully packed in straw in wicker baskets and wheeled along to the goods yard for onward despatch. For a town, though, that continues to derive much of its prosperity from clock making, Whitchurch seems a timeless sort of place, immune to the ebb and flow of fashion.

OLD TOWN HALL VAULTS - St Mary's Street. A Marston's pub which was the birthplace of Sir Edward German, composer of *Merrie England* and other light operatic works. Bar meals available. Tel: 01948 662251.
ETZIO - 60 High Street. Tel: 01948 662248. Smart modern restaurant, evenings only.
JONES COFFEE SHOP - 18 Green End for that espresso fix!
YE OLDE SHOPPE - High Street. Unselfconsciously quaint cafe.
NEW GOLDEN CHEF - Brownlow Street. Tel: 01948 663536. Chinese takeaway - telephone orders welcome.
CHESTERS - Green End. Eat in or take-away fish & chips.

All services in the town centre, one mile east of the canal. Friday is market day, Wednesday early closing. Tesco supermarket by the bus station, plus several good butchers and bakers such as BRADBURY BUTCHERS and WILLIAMS OF WEM, both on High Street; launderette on Station Road. RAW SPIRIT on High Street is a good outlet for organic and speciality foods.

HERITAGE & TOURIST INFORMATION CENTRE - 12 St Mary's Street. Tel: 01948 664577. Nice exhibitions of local history and personalities such as Edward German and the Victorian illustrator Randolph Caldecott.

BUSES - regular service to/from Chester calling at Grindley Brook. One service each way to/from Ellesmere on Wednesdays providing a useful link for would-be towpath walkers. Tel: 0870 608 2 608.
TRAINS - services to Crewe and Shrewsbury. Tel: 08457 484950.

Marbury

One of those 'quietest places under the sun' that we all dream of retiring to. The church lych gate celebrates "Ye who live mid English pastures green". The tiny green has one of those seats which encircles its tree trunk, just begging to be sat upon. Below the village are two meres. A footpath leads down to the larger and you can watch the antics of the resident wildfowl from its reedy banks. Alternatively, there's a secluded seat in the churchyard overlooking the Big Mere. At Gauntons Bank, Norbury, BARN BOOKS deal in new and secondhand books covering a wide range of subjects. Their premises are about quarter of an hour's walk north of Bridge 23 (Map 19). Tel: 01948 663742 for details of opening times etc.

THE SWAN INN - village centre, five minutes walk from Bridges 23 or 24.Tel: 01948 663715.
WILLEY MOOR LOCK - beside the lock. Picturesque - and popular - free house reached by motorists via a track off the A49. Good home cooked meals and snacks and an interesting and ever changing range of ales. Pleasant garden with children's play area. Tel: 01948 663274.

Grindley Brook

HORSE & JOCKEY - just down the B5395 from the locks. Banks's pub serving food. Tel: 01948 662723.
LOCKSIDE STORES (beside the staircase) offer an excellent range of high quality groceries (some organic) perfect for creating effortless dinners or picnics. Local cheeses and meats are complimented by chutneys and jams, as well as crafts, gifts and Tourist Information. Also there's a modern cafe '@29' open from 9am daily offering breakfast, coffees, filled baguettes and teas. Internet access available. Tel: 01948 663385.

SEEMINGLY all alone in the world, the canal crosses remote farmland parallel to the border between Shropshire and the detached part of Clwyd once known as Flintshire.

There are no shops for miles and only one pub - the Waggoners Inn at Platt Lane - anywhere near the canal. With no locks to operate, the boater may be thankful that the occasional lift bridge occupies his attention. All these structures are now built of steel. The wear and tear of passing boats and heavy road traffic have taken its toll on the original wooden structures. The new bridges are also safer to operate, having hydraulically assisted mechanisms instead of the simple, and sometimes unreliable, balance weights of the original bridges.

Bridge 39 carries the decaying trackbed of the once proud Cambrian Railways' Oswestry, Ellesmere and Whitchurch line. Opened in 1863, the route just saw out its centenary before succumbing to the Beeching Axe.

In the summertime it was well used by excursionists bound for the mid Wales coast.

The Llangollen Canal crosses a region of peat mosses - the Fenn's, Whixall and Bettisfield Mosses National Nature Reserve (see Map 22), which represents the third largest lowland raised bog in Britain. For many years commercial peat cutting was carried out here until English Nature acquired the site in the mid 1990s. Now it is once again home to bog rosemary, large heath butterflies, white-faced darter dragonflies and other rare species. There is access to the Reserve from the towpath near Bridge 44. When the canal was built across the mosses early in the 19th century, drainage of the peat caused subsidence and the canal company employed a permanent 'Moss Gang' responsible for raising oak-piled clay embankments. Regrettably, the gang became redundant when steel-piling was introduced in the 1960s.

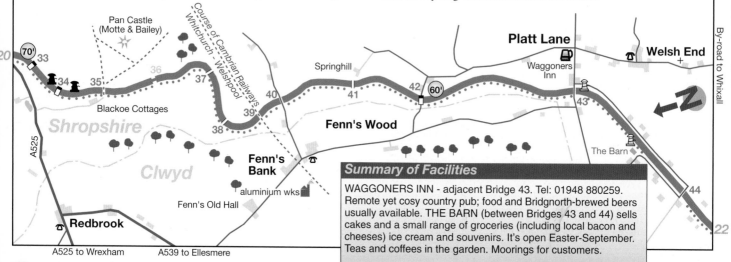

Summary of Facilities

WAGGONERS INN - adjacent Bridge 43. Tel: 01948 880259. Remote yet cosy country pub; food and Bridgnorth-brewed beers usually available. THE BARN (between Bridges 43 and 44) sells cakes and a small range of groceries (including local bacon and cheeses) ice cream and souvenirs. It's open Easter-September. Teas and coffees in the garden. Moorings for customers.

THERE is always something of a 'come hither' element about waterway junctions. However committed you are to the main line a branch seldom fails to tempt you, seeming to dare you to explore whatever languorous charms lie just out of sight. At Whixall the old Prees Branch is no exception, and the remaining mile of what was once a four mile route makes a satisfying diversion from the main canal, often used by discerning boaters for quiet overnight moorings.

Historically, the branch was intended to reach Prees but fell short of its objective by a couple of miles. The actual terminus was established at Quinta Brook. Here a bank of lime burning kilns was erected, for burnt lime was an important farming commodity in the innocent days before chemical fertilizers appeared on the scene. The first, navigable, mile of the Prees Branch serves a marina built on the site of a puddle clay pit from which maintenance men extracted clay to line the canal bed. Beyond the marina its course is now a nature reserve which may be enjoyed - frogbits, yellow water lilies, starworts and all - from the towpath. Two handsome wooden lift bridges survive on the arm. An unusual three-storey canal house watches over Prees Junction, its ground floor lying below the level of the canal. From Moss Farm you can buy fresh meat.

Hampton Bank is one of the Llangollen Canal's lesser sung engineering achievements; it carries the canal perhaps thirty feet above a headwater of the River Roden, a tributary of the Tern which joins the Severn below Shrewsbury. Tall larches mask the bank from the north wind. To the south-east, beyond Wem, stands Grinshill; to the north-west the mountains of Wales. Hampton was another place where lime burning for agriculture took place. L. T. C. Rolt moored at Hampton aboard *Cressy* for a month in the summer of 1947, having been thwarted in an attempt to reach Pontcysyllte because of excessive weed and general decay in the canal beyond Ellesmere.

By-road from Whixall

Course of Prees Branch

Nature Reserve

70'

Whixall Marina

By-road from Whitchurch

Dobson's Bridge

3

2

1

Moss Farm

45

46

Prees Junction

21

Shropshire (England)

Clwyd (Wales)

Fenn's, Whixall & Bettisfield Mosses Nature Reserve

Mosses Trail

47

Cornhill

48

Bettisfield

49

Grinshill

Welsh Hills

53

23

Lyneal Wharf

52

70'

51

50

Hampton Bank

Balmer Heath

N

Shropshire (England)

Ellesmere - 3 miles

Crse of Cambrian Rlys

By-road to A495   By-roads to A495   A495 to Whitchurch

*Time refers to main line, allow 1 hour for return trip along Prees Branch

23 LLANGOLLEN CANAL

T HE old Shropshire town of Ellesmere embraces its eponymous canal emphatically, a robust response to the commerce it continues to bring to the community coffers two centuries after its conception. Yes, it's worth recalling that what we know glibly as the Llangollen Canal is a term which would be unfamiliar to the canal's promoters. For historically this was the Ellesmere Canal, an ambitious attempt to link the rivers Mersey, Dee and Severn with a main line from Chester to Shrewsbury. In the event, only the Pontcysyllte-Weston Lullingfields section was ever built with, from Welsh Frankton (Map 24), branches to Llanymynech and Ellesmere itself. As it became apparent that the intended main line of the canal would never reach the Dee or Severn, the Ellesmere Canal Company *faute de mieux* cut a canal eastwards from Ellesmere to meet the Chester Canal near Nantwich. Hurleston was reached in the year of Trafalgar. Forty years later the Ellesmere Canal amalgamated with the Chester Canal and the new Birmingham & Liverpool Junction Canal to form the Shropshire Union Railways & Canal Company. The route from Hurleston to Llangollen was known as the 'Welsh Section' of the Shropshire Union. The term 'Llangollen Canal' didn't gain general currency until British Waterways published a cruising guide under that name in 1956.

Ellesmere became the headquarters of the canal and the company built imposing offices here. Known

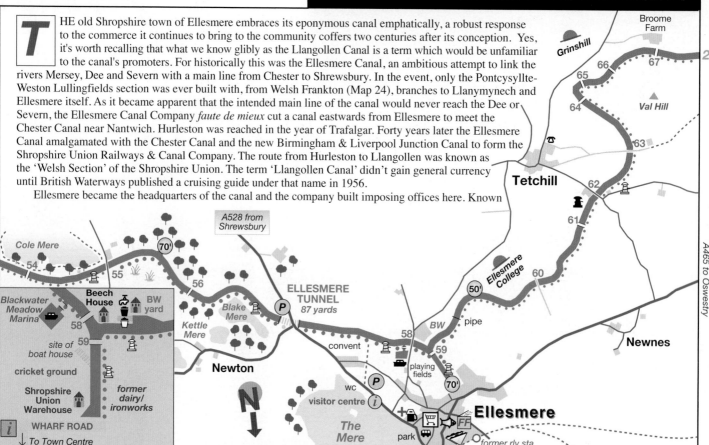

A528 to Wrexham   B5068 to St Martin's

as Beech House, these premises still preside over the canal junction, though used residentially now, British Waterways having their offices amidst the charming higgledy-piggledy maintenance base next door. Many of the structures which comprise this yard date back to the earliest years of the canal. Particularly notable is the handsome stone drydock with distinctive weathervane in the shape of a narrowboat atop its slate roof. Workshops of timber and stone construction include a joiner's shop, blacksmith's forge and pattern store where wooden templates used for making accurate moulds for iron castings are kept.

Opposite Beech House a short arm leads to the town wharf. Twenty years ago this was the best place to moor in Ellesmere. Now, overlooked by a derelict creamery and a decaying Shropshire Union warehouse which cries out for refurbishment, there is a lugubrious ambience about the arm which reflects unfairly on the community. Fair enough, the towpath has been metalled, and there are bins provided in which the more scrupulous of dog-walkers can deposit their pets's droppings, but something needs to be done to bring life back to this quietly languishing corner of the town.

East of Ellesmere the Llangollen Canal undertakes a hauntingly lovely journey through Shropshire's own 'lakeland'. There are seven lakes, or meres, in the neighbourhood of Ellesmere without inflow or outflow. They were formed at the end of the Ice Age, 10,000 years ago, as the great glaciers retreated and melted waters collected in cups of the land. The meres support a resident population of birds including kingfishers, herons, grebe, Canada geese, coots and moorhens. In winter there's an influx of wildfowl - widgeon, teal, pochard, greylag geese and cormorants. On hot late summer evenings the phenomenon of 'breaking' occurs, as algae rise from the depths to spread a deep blue-green veil upon the surface. Cole Mere and Blake Mere both lie beside the canal, the latter only separated from the waterway by a narrow belt of trees which provide shade for picnics on warm summer days. Forget the helter-skelter rush towards Llangollen, this is one of the true highlights of the canal, a place to linger, unwind and find a real sense of peace. The unique charm of the meres was evoked in Mary Webb's 1926 novel *Precious Bane*.

Westwards, the canal rapidly escapes into empty countryside, skirting the playing fields of Ellesmere College, a Woodard boarding school, and the shop-less, pub-less village of Tetchill.

Ellesmere

Ellesmere is a rare survival, a small, unspoilt country town with no pretensions. Life seems as slowly lived here as the rhythmic lapping of waters on the shores of the meres. Visitors - whether they come by car to feed the ducks, or by boat along the Llangollen Canal - are assimilated without the usual symptomatic rash of tourist traps. Ellesmere's is a long history, traceable back to the Iron Age. The local economy has traditionally been an agricultural one, once there was an ironworks, an important railway junction and a rennet factory, but what the visitor sees today is a late 19th century country town preserved almost in aspic, and all very delightful it is too!

 BLACK LION HOTEL - Scotland Street. Bar and restaurant food. Tel: 01691 622418.
PETE'S SANDWICH BAR - Cross Street. Down to earth cafe featuring Vermeulen pies and pastries. Tel: 01691 623414.
THE CELLAR - High Street. Homely restaurant in the brick-vaulted basement of the old Town Hall. Tel : 01691 622433.
WHITE HART - Birch Road. Ancient Marston's/Border house. Tel: 01691 622333.
KEBAB & PIZZA HOUSE - Cross Street. Tel: 01691 624638. Free local delivery service.

Shopping is the pleasantest of experiences in this lovely old town, the highlight, to our mind, being Vermeulens delicatessen on Cross Street (Tel: 01691 622521) by the town square. They open around seven in the morning, by which time the aroma of their baking has wafted down to the canal wharf. Their pork pies, still warm to the touch by mid-morning, are simply irresistible, whilst the cold counter contains a mouthwatering array of glazed meats, pates, shellfish and cheeses. Get them to grind some coffee beans for you then dare yourself to leave without a box of their fresh cream cakes. The indoor market, housed in a handsome Victorian pile opposite the post office, operates on Tuesdays. Thursday is half day. There are several banks in the town. Craft and antique shops feature largely, and you will do well to cast off without some tangible souvenir and a corresponding deficit in your credit card balance.

 TOURIST INFORMATION - Wharf Road. Tel: 01691 624488. Info Link, Wharf Road - Tel: 01691 624488.
MERES VISITOR CENTRE - Mereside. Rowing boats for hire on the Mere. Tel: 01691 622981.
BUSES - regular services to Oswestry; less frequently to Whitchurch and Wem. Tel: 0870 608 2 608.

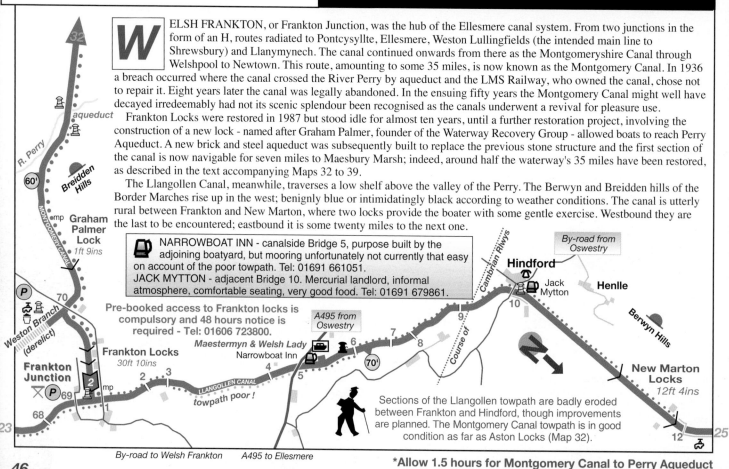

WELSH FRANKTON, or Frankton Junction, was the hub of the Ellesmere canal system. From two junctions in the form of an H, routes radiated to Pontcysyllte, Ellesmere, Weston Lullingfields (the intended main line to Shrewsbury) and Llanymynech. The canal continued onwards from there as the Montgomeryshire Canal through Welshpool to Newtown. This route, amounting to some 35 miles, is now known as the Montgomery Canal. In 1936 a breach occurred where the canal crossed the River Perry by aqueduct and the LMS Railway, who owned the canal, chose not to repair it. Eight years later the canal was legally abandoned. In the ensuing fifty years the Montgomery Canal might well have decayed irredeemably had not its scenic splendour been recognised as the canals underwent a revival for pleasure use.

Frankton Locks were restored in 1987 but stood idle for almost ten years, until a further restoration project, involving the construction of a new lock - named after Graham Palmer, founder of the Waterway Recovery Group - allowed boats to reach Perry Aqueduct. A new brick and steel aqueduct was subsequently built to replace the previous stone structure and the first section of the canal is now navigable for seven miles to Maesbury Marsh; indeed, around half the waterway's 35 miles have been restored, as described in the text accompanying Maps 32 to 39.

The Llangollen Canal, meanwhile, traverses a low shelf above the valley of the Perry. The Berwyn and Breidden hills of the Border Marches rise up in the west; benignly blue or intimidatingly black according to weather conditions. The canal is utterly rural between Frankton and New Marton, where two locks provide the boater with some gentle exercise. Westbound they are the last to be encountered; eastbound it is some twenty miles to the next one.

NARROWBOAT INN - canalside Bridge 5, purpose built by the adjoining boatyard, but mooring unfortunately not currently that easy on account of the poor towpath. Tel: 01691 661051.
JACK MYTTON - adjacent Bridge 10. Mercurial landlord, informal atmosphere, comfortable seating, very good food. Tel: 01691 679861.

Pre-booked access to Frankton locks is compulsory and 48 hours notice is required - Tel: 01606 723800.

Sections of the Llangollen towpath are badly eroded between Frankton and Hindford, though improvements are planned. The Montgomery Canal towpath is in good condition as far as Aston Locks (Map 32).

aqueduct

R. Perry

Breidden Hills

Graham Palmer Lock
1ft 9ins

MONTGOMERY CANAL

Weston Branch
(derelict)

Frankton Junction

Frankton Locks
30ft 10ins

LLANGOLLEN CANAL
towpath poor !

Maestermyn & Welsh Lady
Narrowboat Inn

A495 from Oswestry

Hindford

Jack Mytton

By-road from Oswestry

Henlle

Berwyn Hills

Course of Cambrian Rlwys

New Marton Locks
12ft 4ins

By-road to Welsh Frankton   A495 to Ellesmere

***Allow 1.5 hours for Montgomery Canal to Perry Aqueduct**

Welsh Frankton

47

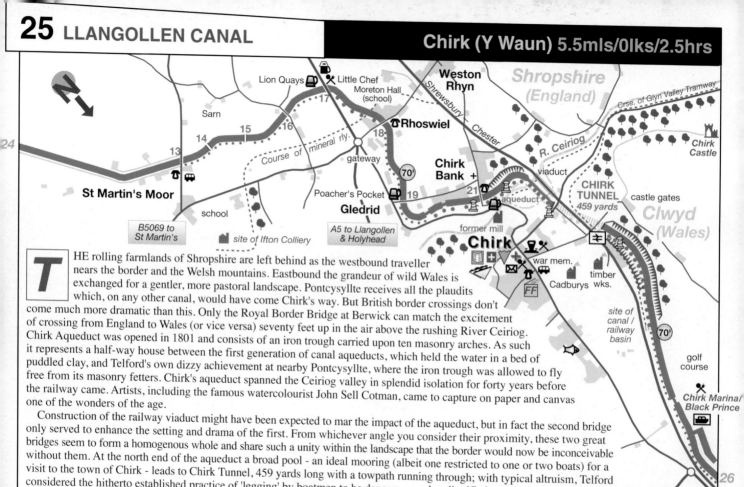

Lion Quays
Little Chef
Moreton Hall (school)
Sarn
Rhoswiel
Weston Rhyn
Shropshire (England)
Crse. of Glyn Valley Tramway
24
14
15
16
13
Course of mineral rly.
gateway
18
17
Shrewsbury ~ Chester
R. Ceiriog
Chirk Castle
St Martin's Moor
school
70'
Chirk Bank
viaduct
CHIRK TUNNEL 459 yards
castle gates
Clwyd (Wales)
B5069 to St Martin's
site of Ifton Colliery
Poacher's Pocket
19
Gledrid
A5 to Llangollen & Holyhead
21
aqueduct
former mill
Chirk
war mem.
Cadburys
FF
timber wks.
site of canal / railway basin
70'
golf course
Chirk Marina/ Black Prince

THE rolling farmlands of Shropshire are left behind as the westbound traveller nears the border and the Welsh mountains. Eastbound the grandeur of wild Wales is exchanged for a gentler, more pastoral landscape. Pontcysyllte receives all the plaudits which, on any other canal, would have come Chirk's way. But British border crossings don't come much more dramatic than this. Only the Royal Border Bridge at Berwick can match the excitement of crossing from England to Wales (or vice versa) seventy feet up in the air above the rushing River Ceiriog. Chirk Aqueduct was opened in 1801 and consists of an iron trough carried upon ten masonry arches. As such it represents a half-way house between the first generation of canal aqueducts, which held the water in a bed of puddled clay, and Telford's own dizzy achievement at nearby Pontcysyllte, where the iron trough was allowed to fly free from its masonry fetters. Chirk's aqueduct spanned the Ceiriog valley in splendid isolation for forty years before the railway came. Artists, including the famous watercolourist John Sell Cotman, came to capture on paper and canvas one of the wonders of the age.

Construction of the railway viaduct might have been expected to mar the impact of the aqueduct, but in fact the second bridge only served to enhance the setting and drama of the first. From whichever angle you consider their proximity, these two great bridges seem to form a homogenous whole and share such a unity within the landscape that the border would now be inconceivable without them. At the north end of the aqueduct a broad pool - an ideal mooring (albeit one restricted to one or two boats) for a visit to the town of Chirk - leads to Chirk Tunnel, 459 yards long with a towpath running through; with typical altruism, Telford considered the hitherto established practice of 'legging' by boatmen to be dangerous and undignified.

A5 to Shrewsbury

Chirk Arches

Beyond the northern portal of Chirk Tunnel the canal penetrates a wooded cutting of some magnitude. At its far end a winding hole marks the site of a former transhipment wharf between the canal and the narrow gauge Glyn Valley Tramway. Sadly, this was one of the 'Great Little Trains of Wales' which ran out of steam before the era of railway preservation. Built to serve mines and quarries at the head of the Ceiriog Valley, it also carried passengers. From a separate station alongside the main line, the track curved precipitously down to the valley floor and then ran beside what is now the B4500. The line closed in 1935. Had it survived the war, it might have been another Talyllyn, for L. T. C. Rolt, a leading light in the rescue of that railway, also held the Glyn Valley Tramway dear to his heart.

Chirk

Many boaters do not bother to visit Chirk, anxious to push on to Pontcysyllte and Llangollen. A pity, because the village centre contains an interesting selection of buildings, including the parish church of St Mary's, the remains of a motte and bailey castle, an old coaching inn recalling the heyday of Telford's A5 (which now bypasses the village) and a war memorial of Portland stone carved by sculptor and typographer Eric Gill - look out for the wrought iron sculpture depicting a boat and train on the bridges on the park gate opposite, and the plaque commemorating Billy Meredith, born here in 1874, the 'wing wizard' who won the Welsh Cup with Chirk FC and went on to play for both Manchester clubs and his country on many occasions. Once a mining community, Chirk is now dominated by the Cadbury plant and adjoining Kronospan timber works, whilst in the woods between the railway and the canal, where once the diminutive engines of the GVR shunted back and forth, stands a small estate of industrial units.

THE CHIRK TANDOORI - Station Avenue. Tel: 01691 772499. Popular Indian restaurant.
THE HAND HOTEL - Church Street. Ancient coaching inn with buttery bar and more formal restaurant. Tel: 01691 773472.
THE CLUB HOUSE - bar and restaurant adjunct to marina and golf course. Tel: 01691 774407.
BRIDGE INN - Banks's pub located beneath the canal embankment. Tel: 01691 773213.
POACHER'S POCKET - canalside Bridge19. Tel: 01691 773250.
LION QUAYS - canalside Bridge 17. Tel: 01691 684300. Stylish new establishment thoughtfully providing mooring pontoons for boating patrons, an example beyond the neighbouring Little Chef.
Butcher (offering delicious hot roast baps), chemist, and a Co-op (with cash-back) cater for most pressing needs in the centre of Chirk, and there's also a branch of the HSBC Bank.
CHIRK CASTLE - Just over a mile from the north end of the tunnel. Admission charge for non National Trust members. Open daily Apr-Nov (ex Mons & Tues) Tel: 01691 777701.
BUSES - Bryn Melyn services to/from Llangollen via Froncysyllte. Tel: 01978 860701.
Arriva Midland services to/from Oswestry and Wrexham. Tel: 0870 608 2 608.
TRAINS - Regular services to/from Chester and Shrewsbury. Tel: 08457 484950.

Map labels

A5 from Llangollen

A539 from Llangollen

27

36

35

34

Crse of GWR: Barmouth-Ruabon

Trevor Hall

Offa's Dyke F/p

Plas-yn-Pentre

Garth Trevor

N

Fron Isaf

Froncysyllte

33

32

31

Trevor

P

70'

28

Pontcysyllte Aqueduct

29

site of canal / railway basin

chemical wks.

site of quarry wharf

R. Dee

Offa's Dyke Footpath

Offa's Dyke Footpath

aqueduct

Offa's Dyke

26

25

27

WHITEHOUSES TUNNEL
191 yards

Newbridge Viaduct

Pentre

B5605 to Ruabon

To Llangollen

To Chirk

aqueduct

steps down to river

drydock

Anglo Welsh

The Telford

70'

P

Body text

ENTERING Offa's Dyke country, the Llangollen Canal prepares to make its most dramatic gesture. But first westbound travellers are treated to another tunnel followed by an enchanted passage through a mask of woodland on a shelf above the River Dee. Given the right conditions, the delicious aroma of pinewood fills the air. Between the ivy clad boles of the tall trees there are glimpses of an impressive railway viaduct. Like the canal builders before them, the railway engineers had to contend with the deep valley of the Dee. On the outskirts of Froncysyllte the remains of the former Pen-y-Graig limestone quarries are evident alongside the canal. The actual quarry faces lay uphill to the west and the stone was brought down by a series of tramway inclines on wagons. The tops of six limekilns were at road level with the bottom exits beside the canal. Passing Bridge 28 the canal approaches its climax on a huge embankment built from spoil excavated when Chirk Tunnel was dug.

Pontcysyllte Aqueduct, the most astonishing feat of canal engineering in the world, carries the canal one hundred and twenty feet high across the creaming waters of the River Dee. Superlatives are superfluous, but what is surprising is that the aqueduct is relatively unknown beyond the narrow world of the waterways. It ought to be as familiar as Big Ben and Alton Towers, yet few people are aware of its existence, let alone able to get their teeth around its knotty consonants. But, pronounced 'Pont-ker-sulth-tee', the bare facts are that it is over 1,000 feet long, 127 feet tall at its deepest point, and consists of an iron trough supported by 18 stone piers. The aqueduct was completed in 1805, the year of Nelson's death at Trafalgar. Along with the Menai suspension bridge, it is ranked among Telford's most outstanding achievements.

At Trevor, the canal was to have carried on over the ridge now occupied by the huge chemical plant and then down through Wrexham to the Dee at Chester. Such a course would have required many locks, a very long tunnel or a series of boat lifts. The enormity of this undertaking, coupled with the recession which occurred as an aftermath to the Napoleonic Wars, thwarted the Ellesmere Canal Company's plans to provide a direct canal between the Mersey and the Severn. Telford and his associates would doubtless have overcome the terrain in time, but financially the outlay involved would have broken the bank. In place of the envisaged main line northwards, the canal beyond the aqueduct terminated at a transhipment wharf from where, first a tramway, then later a railway, connected with quarries and collieries on the higher ground towards Ruabon. A further arm described an arc to the east serving chemical, pottery and iron works in the vicinity. In the Ellesmere Canal's commercial heyday much traffic was generated in the neighbourhood.

Ironically, a canal to Llangollen was not originally planned. Only when it became clear that the main line would never be completed did the company decide to provide a feeder from the River Dee at Llantisilio to the canal at Trevor. The cutting of a canal along the steep slopes of the Vale of Llangollen posed considerable problems and this was the last section of the canal to be completed, over two years after the aqueduct had been opened to traffic. Technicalities apart, it is one of the most memorable lengths of canal in the country, an aquatic mountain odyssey of unparalleled loveliness.

Pontcysyllte Aqueduct

Froncysyllte

A mountain goat of a village, with, now that we are in Wales, a fair sprinkling of Nonconformist chapels. If your legs are up to it, it's worth following the zig-zagging lane up to the crest of the ridge for spectacular views across the Dee Valley and up into the Vale of Llangollen.

A roadside pub called THE AQUEDUCT and an Indian take-away (Tel: 01691 774858) are all that 'Fron' currently offers to passers-by, be they on the Holyhead road or the canal to Llangollen.

BUSES - Bryn Melyn services to/from Llangollen and Chirk, Ruabon and Wrexham. Tel: 01978 266166.

Trevor

Industry spills down the hillside and the basin is hard by a housing estate, but the canal shrugs off such intrusions and a large car park reflects the popularity of the aqueduct as a visitor attraction.

TELFORD INN - Tel: 01978 820469. Canalside next to the Anglo Welsh hire base. Understandably popular with both boaters and land based visitors, the 'Telford' offers Tetley's real ales and an excellent range of food. Families welcome. Canalside seating area and a children's playground. A couple of other pubs up in Trevor on the A539 road to Llangollen.

There is a small general store and off licence some 200 yards from the canal basin, whilst groceries, gifts, cards, guides and maps are available from the Anglo Welsh boatyard shop.

BUSES - Arriva Cymru service to/from Llangollen and Wrexham from stops on the A539. Tel: 0870 608 2 608.

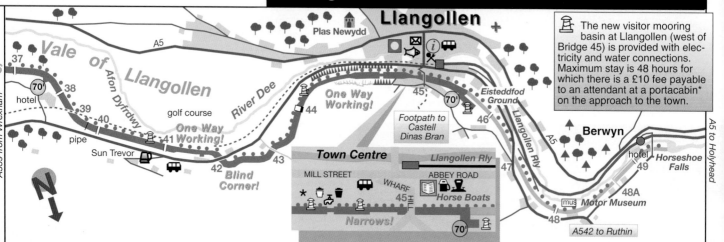

The new visitor mooring basin at Llangollen (west of Bridge 45) is provided with electricity and water connections. Maximum stay is 48 hours for which there is a £10 fee payable to an attendant at a portacabin* on the approach to the town.

AFTER the high (literally and metaphorically) drama of Pontcysyllte you might have expected the last lap into Llangollen to be something of an anticlimax. Happily, this is not the case; rather, the canal treats you to all the wild majesty that the celebrated Vale of Llangollen can muster. Great buttresses of limestone cliffs tower above conifer plantations, making Hurleston and gentle green Cheshire seem an eternity away. When the weather is kind, you find yourself constantly lifting your eyes up into the hills, where sunlight gives the heather-clad ridges the clarity of well executed marquetry. But Wales wouldn't be Wales if it weren't for the frequent, dripping Celtic mists that come creeping up the valley of the Dee, muffling boat exhausts and dampening the woods, but not the spirits.

Not surprisingly, the section between Trevor and Llangollen has a history of breaches. In 1945 the bank collapsed by Bridge 41 and the adjoining

railway was swept away. A goods train plunged into the gap and the driver was killed. Bursts occurred more frequently thereafter and by the mid Eighties it became apparent to British Waterways that this section would, effectively, have to be rebuilt. Nowadays the canal bed is concrete-lined, under drained and fitted with a waterproof membrane following an extensive improvement programme.

Never exactly wide, the canal narrows as it approaches Llangollen with 'one way working' along three short sections. Boaters need to be patient in high season, and a good deal of frustration can be saved by sending a member of your party ahead to check if a boat is approaching in the opposite direction.

Running above the grey roofs of the town the canal reaches the old Llangollen wharf where the warehouse serves as a base for the horse-drawn boats which ply the final, narrow, shallow section up to

Horseshoe Falls. A winding hole beyond the warehouse marks the turning point for all powered craft.

Finally, accompanied by the River Dee and the gently puffing trains of the restored steam railway, the feeder canal continues for another couple of miles beyond Llangollen to Llantisilio. In many ways it seems entirely appropriate that boaters should have to stretch their legs to reach what amounts to the end - but is really the beginning - of the canal. Horseshoe Falls, though, with its great crescent shaped weir, overlooked by the bulk of Llantisilio Mountain and the higher peaks of the Berwyns, is a point of pilgrimage which should not be eschewed. Here, by the tiny valve house that meters the flow of water into the canal, it is time to savour the forty-four mile journey from Hurleston. To recall with affection the green pastures of the Cheshire plain; the mellow mills of Wrenbury; the staircase locks at Grindley Brook; the strange mosses; the lonely Prees Branch; the gently lapping meres; the bold, bare mountains; the spectacular aqueducts at Chirk and Pontcysyllte. All the ingredients, in fact, which taken together, make the Llangollen Canal one of the great inland waterway experiences in the world.

Llangollen

Once a year in early July, this little grey-slated Welsh town takes on a cosmopolitan atmosphere, as singers and dancers in colourful national dress take part in the famous Eisteddfod. In fact, the town is busy with tourists all summer long, as it has been since the 18th century, when early travel writers like Hazlitt and Borrow discovered the wild charm of the Vale of Llangollen. Arguably, Llangollen's heyday coincided with the residence here of the 'Ladies of Llangollen' when such august figures as Wordsworth, Sir Walter Scott and the Duke of Wellington were regular visitors. The canal wharf lies over the river from the bulk of the town, but it's just a short walk across the graceful Bishop Trevor Bridge to the centre.

THE CORN MILL - Dee Lane. Tel: 01978 869555. Look no further than this stylish modern restaurant & bar housed within an 18th century mill whose water wheel still turns for the entertainment of diners. Balcony seating for warm days with views across the Dee to the comings and goings of Llangollen's steam trains.

GALES WINE BAR - Bridge Street. Tel: 01978 860089. Characterful wine bar offering food and also accommodation.

CHAIN BRIDGE HOTEL - canalside Bridge 49. Tel: 01978 860215. Bar and restaurant food for non-residents with views over the Dee at 'un-navigable' end of the canal.

SUN - Regent Street, A5. Tel: 01928 860233. CAMRA recommended drinking den.

SUN TREVOR - adjacent Bridge 41. Pleasant roadside pub with good moorings available away from the crush at Llangollen. Tel: 01928 860651.

Predictably, there's a surfeit of gift shops, yet in amongst all the dross there are many genuinely attractive craft outlets. Plenty of good food shops too, notably the JAMES BAILEY'S delicatessen (offering hugely tasty Welsh Oggies) and the butcher D.M. PIERSON, both on Castle Street. Market day is Tuesday, there are branches of NatWest, Barclays and HSBC banks, and you'll find a useful launderette on Regent Street, the A5.

TOURIST INFORMATION CENTRE - The Chapel, Castle Street. Tel: 01978 860828.

LLANGOLLEN WHARF - The Wharf. Tel: 01978 860702. Base for motor-boat and horse-drawn trip boats. Gift shop and cafe.

LLANGOLLEN BIKE HIRE - Castle Street. Tel: 01928 860605.

LLANGOLLEN MUSEUM - Parade Street. Tel: 01978 862862.

LLANGOLLEN RAILWAY - station riverside, next to the canal wharf. Daily service (May to October) of steam hauled trains through delightful Dee Valley scenery to Carrog. Combined rail/boat trips. Gift shop and refreshment room at station overlooking the Dee. Tel: 01978 860979/860951.

PLAS NEWYDD - Hill Street. This delightful black and white timbered house set in charming gardens was the home of the 'Ladies of Llangollen', two daughters of aristocratic Irish families who lived here from 1779 to 1831. Admission charge. Open daily Easter to October. Tel: 01978 861314. And all around are the hills, just begging to be climbed. A particularly fine walk leads from Bridge 45 to the 1000ft summit of Castell Dinas Bran.

BUSES - Bryn Melin services to/from Chirk. Tel: 01978 860701. Arriva Cymru services to/from Wrexham, Corwen, Bala and Barmouth. Tel: 0870 608 2 608.

The **MIDDLEWICH** *Branch*

Church Minshull 4.5mls/0lks/1.5hrs

TO subconsciously relegate the Middlewich Branch to the back of your mind as an unspectacular but necessary link in the waterways of the North-west would be unjust, for this is a rumbustious canal, carrying you loftily above the snaking valley of the River Weaver, and presenting you with expansive views towards a horizon bounded by Delamere Forest and the Peckforton Hills. Church Minshull looks - from the canal's elevated position - like a toy village embracing the river's luxuriant banks. Tom and Angela Rolt enjoyed an extended stay here in the fateful autumn of 1939 while Tom worked for Rolls-Royce at Crewe.

Keep your eyes peeled for the Jacobean style house alongside Bridge 14. Between bridges 18 and 19 former canal horse stables have been fetchingly refurbished as living quarters after years lying derelict. Note how the adjoining canal cottage boasts three storeys to the rear. Several sizeable farms border the canal, their fields filled with black and white milking herds or cut red by the plough in a ruddy shade of corduroy. Near Bridge 22, woods partially obscure the Top Flash, a subsidence induced lake beside the Weaver. The West Coast Main Line, busy with silver-coloured Virgin trains for the most part, crosses the canal. To the south-east lies a forgotten, older transport route, a Roman road which linked the early salt mines at Nantwich and Middlewich.

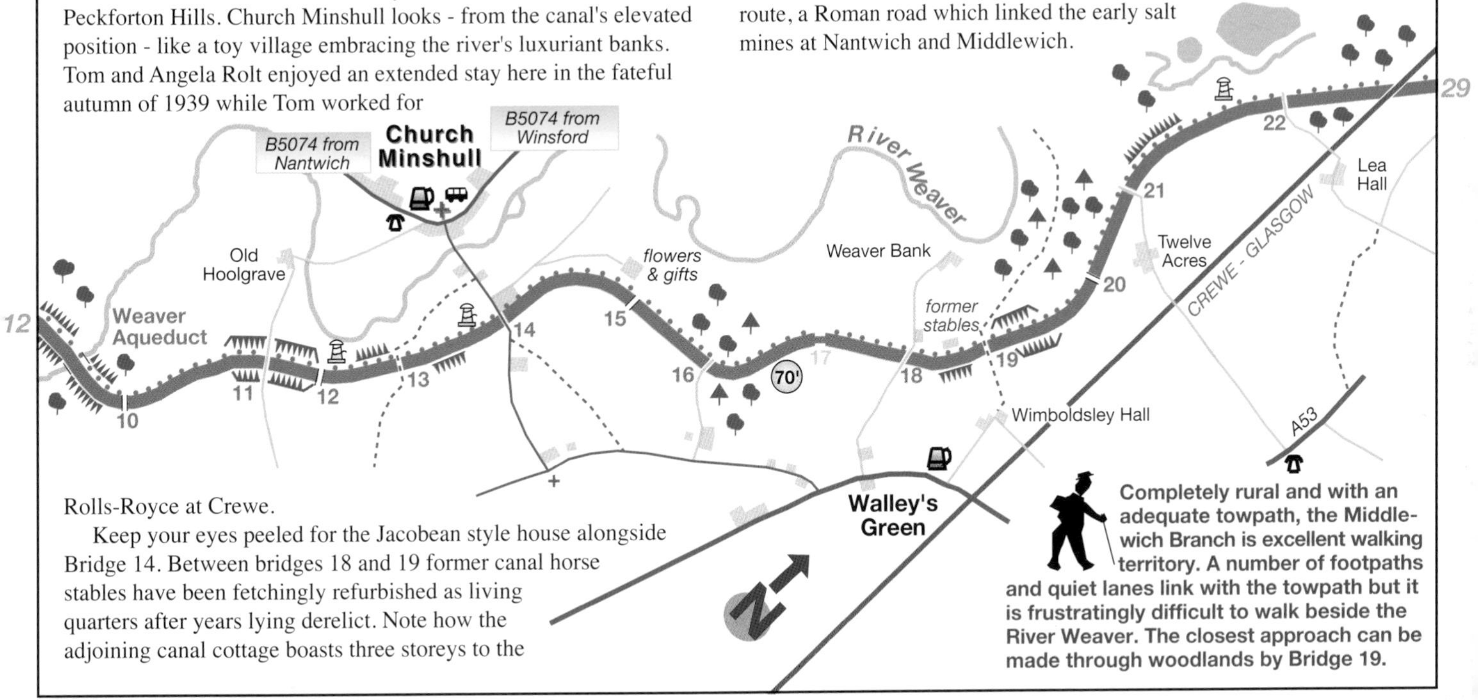

B5074 from Nantwich
Church Minshull
B5074 from Winsford
River Weaver
Weaver Bank
Old Hoolgrave
Weaver Aqueduct
flowers & gifts
former stables
Twelve Acres
Lea Hall
CREWE - GLASGOW
Wimboldsley Hall
A53
Walley's Green
70'
10
11
12
13
14
15
16
17
18
19
20
21
22
12
29

Completely rural and with an adequate towpath, the Middlewich Branch is excellent walking territory. A number of footpaths and quiet lanes link with the towpath but it is frustratingly difficult to walk beside the River Weaver. The closest approach can be made through woodlands by Bridge 19.

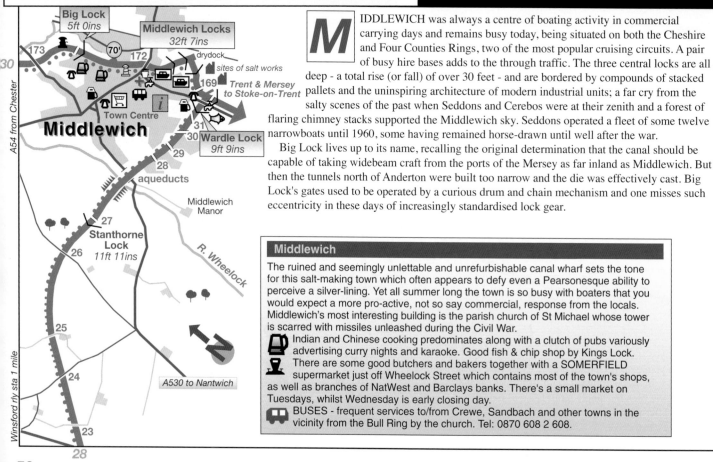

MIDDLEWICH was always a centre of boating activity in commercial carrying days and remains busy today, being situated on both the Cheshire and Four Counties Rings, two of the most popular cruising circuits. A pair of busy hire bases adds to the through traffic. The three central locks are all deep - a total rise (or fall) of over 30 feet - and are bordered by compounds of stacked pallets and the uninspiring architecture of modern industrial units; a far cry from the salty scenes of the past when Seddons and Cerebos were at their zenith and a forest of flaring chimney stacks supported the Middlewich sky. Seddons operated a fleet of some twelve narrowboats until 1960, some having remained horse-drawn until well after the war.

Big Lock lives up to its name, recalling the original determination that the canal should be capable of taking widebeam craft from the ports of the Mersey as far inland as Middlewich. But then the tunnels north of Anderton were built too narrow and the die was effectively cast. Big Lock's gates used to be operated by a curious drum and chain mechanism and one misses such eccentricity in these days of increasingly standardised lock gear.

Middlewich

The ruined and seemingly unlettable and unrefurbishable canal wharf sets the tone for this salt-making town which often appears to defy even a Pearsonesque ability to perceive a silver-lining. Yet all summer long the town is so busy with boaters that you would expect a more pro-active, not so say commercial, response from the locals. Middlewich's most interesting building is the parish church of St Michael whose tower is scarred with missiles unleashed during the Civil War.

Indian and Chinese cooking predominates along with a clutch of pubs variously advertising curry nights and karaoke. Good fish & chip shop by Kings Lock.

There are some good butchers and bakers together with a SOMERFIELD supermarket just off Wheelock Street which contains most of the town's shops, as well as branches of NatWest and Barclays banks. There's a small market on Tuesdays, whilst Wednesday is early closing day.

BUSES - frequent services to/from Crewe, Sandbach and other towns in the vicinity from the Bull Ring by the church. Tel: 0870 608 2 608.

WOODLAND interludes and subsidence-induced flashes characterise the Trent & Mersey's serene passage through the Dane Valley. Hereabouts the river (having risen in the Derbyshire Peak District on the flanks of Axe Edge) has grown sluggish with age and meanders about its level valley in a succession of broad loops. One moment it is hard by the canal, the next across the pasturelands of milking herds. The soil here is soft and the Dane carves deep banks shadowed by alder and willow. The canal shares the valley with a Roman Road known as King Street and a now lightly-used railway which once carried a push & pull service between Crewe and Northwich, but these other transport modes barely intrude on what is otherwise a long, relaxing pound.

The most curious features of this section are the flashes bordering the main channel to the south of Bridge 181. That nearest the bridge was once filled with the submerged wrecks of abandoned narrowboats, an inland waterway equivalent of Scapa Flow. Many of the boats were brought here and sunk en masse during the Fifties in circumstances almost as controversial in canal terms as the scuttling of the German fleet at Scapa after the First World War. In what was probably a book-keeping exercise, British Waterways rid themselves of surplus narrowboats in a number of watery graves throughout the system. In recent years the wrecks have been raised and taken off for restoration. One generation's cast-offs become the next's prized possessions.

Whatcroft Hall is topped by a handsome dome. By Bridge 179 its old lodge houses are prettily half-timbered. In the woods between bridges 176 and 177 the mangled remains of old wagon tipplers hint at the existence of clay or puddle pits. Note also how the bridges along this length are flat topped so that they could be relatively easily raised in the event of subsidence.

Croxton Aqueduct was rebuilt to broad beam dimensions in 1891 so as to permit widebeam craft to work between Anderton and Middlewich, but after being damaged by flooding in the Thirties, it was rebuilt to its present narrow status.

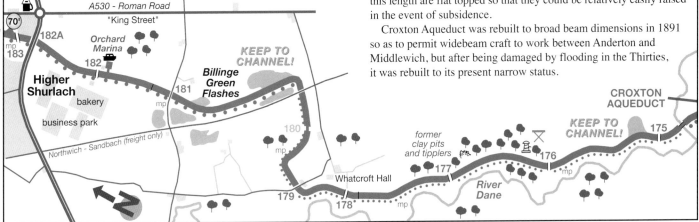

WINCHAM and Anderton introduce industry to this section of the Trent & Mersey but some canal travellers may welcome the intrusion of factories into the peaceful landscape; variety being the spice of life, after all.

This part of Cheshire was the centre of Britain's salt industry and the canal negotiates a scarred landscape destabilised over the years by salt extraction. In 1958 a new length of canal had to be dug at Marston to by-pass a section bedevilled by subsidence. LION SALT WORKS was the last in Britain to produce salt by the traditional method of evaporating brine in open pans. It closed in 1986 but is now gradually being restored as a working museum and visitor centre.

Now, happily, fully restored, the Anderton Boat Lift dates from 1875, being designed by eminent Victorian engineer Sir Edward Leader-Williams. The Lift was constructed to bridge the 50 foot disparity between the Trent & Mersey and the Weaver Navigation below. A massive framework supports two water-filled caissons, each of which can carry a pair of narrowboats. The structure was originally hydraulically powered by steam, but was later electrically operated using a system of counterbalance weights. Of all the so called 'Seven Wonders of the Waterways', Anderton Lift is arguably the most ingenious, which makes it all the more welcome that it is back in business.

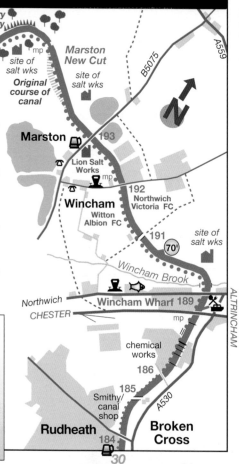

Anderton

The Lift makes Anderton a household name in waterway circles; otherwise it has little of note, being a dull suburb of Northwich, to where bus service E55 runs at frequent intervals.

THE MOORINGS - Anderton Marina. Tel: 01606 79789. Restaurant and coffee shop popular with boaters.

STANLEY ARMS - canalside opposite lift. Tel: 01606 75059.

SALT BARGE by Bridge 193 serves Burtonwood ales and bar meals. Tel: 01606 43064.

ⓘ LION SALT WORKS - Bridge 193. Gradually being restored, the site is open daily, whilst an indoor exhibition and shop is open most afternoons. Tel: 01606 41823.

ANDERTON LIFT - Visitor Centre. Tel: 01606 786777. The Lift and its history. Boat trips up and down!

The
MONTGOMERY
Canal

HOWEVER popular the Montgomery Canal may become, as restoration forges ahead, its topographical hinterland will remain remote, creating a welcome sense of isolation. After a burst of activity generated by Frankton Locks, the junction with the intended main line to Shrewsbury, Graham Palmer Lock and the new aqueduct over the River Perry (see Map 24), the canal soon loses itself in a timeless agricultural landscape, the Berwyn and Breidden hills defining the western horizon. Accommodation bridges are conspicuous by their absence. Perhaps the canal followed the boundary between farms.

At Heath Houses the Shrewsbury-Chester railway crosses the canal and a derelict arm extends into the reedy precincts of a former transhipment basin, used in latter years as a bone works. In the mid 19th century a short-lived packet boat service operated between Newtown and Heath Houses to connect with the railway, whose high-chimnied station house is still visible up on the embankment to the south.

The quaint looking brick and timber building abutting Bridge 74 was a passenger terminal for users of the packet. Apparently the Wolverhampton Swift Packet Boat Company advertised a schedule of just over five hours for their boat to cover the 32 miles and 22 locks involved!

Running parallel to a busy by-road, and skirting the edge of a wood of silver birch, the canal makes its quiet way to Queens Head, a small roadside community on Telford's road to Holyhead, the A5. In the canal's working days there were mills here and a sand wharf linked to a narrow gauge railway. From 1996 to 2003 this marked a temporary terminus in restoration terms. Aston Locks had been restored for use by boats, but controversy surrounded the passage of the canal through an area designated as being of Special Scientific Interest on account of the rare plants and insects which thrive here. The resultant truce involves responsibilities on the part of passing boaters.

The towpath is in good condition between Frankton Junction and Aston Locks, comfortable for walkers and cyclists alike. Thereafter it deteriorates somewhat: walkable, but bumpy for cyclists.

Queens Head

The QUEENS HEAD - canalside Bridge 76. Refurbished 'all-day' pub serving a wide choice of food and real ales, including Wood's Shropshire beers. Tel: 01691 610255.

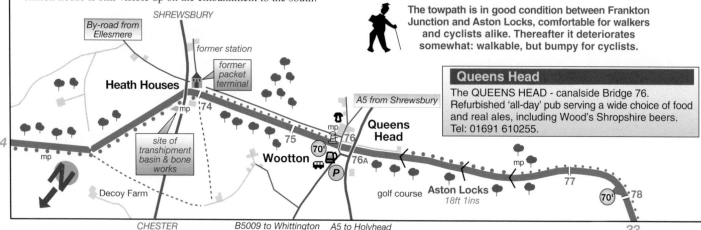

SHREWSBURY

By-road from Ellesmere

former station

former packet terminal

Heath Houses

24

A5 from Shrewsbury

Queens Head

Wootton

site of transhipment basin & bone works

Decoy Farm

golf course

Aston Locks
18ft 1ins

77

78

33

CHESTER   B5009 to Whittington   A5 to Holyhead

REVELLING in its rural isolation, the Montgomery Canal comes upon Maesbury Marsh, a quintessential country wharf with an inn, stables, boatmen's cottages and dock with crane; the waterway equivalent of a country station before the Beeching era. Business used to be brisk at Maesbury Marsh, for this was the nearest wharf to Oswestry, and many commodities came and went through here before the railway reached the town. Sycamore House, the agent's residence, bears a family likeness to Beech House back at Ellesmere.

Bridge 81 is a newly provided lifting structure. Beyond it the short arm which once led to Peates Mill has been re-invigorated by Maesbury Wharf Cruisers. Sadly, the mill ceased operating in 2002 - though Lloyd's more modern animal feeds plant continues to be very much in business near Bridge 83. Peates once operated their own fleet of narrowboats, having purchased eleven craft from the Shropshire Union Company when they ceased trading in 1921. Soon, though, the development of the motor lorry made it unviable to continue carrying by canal. The grain Peates imported by way of Ellesmere Port took three or four days to reach the mill by boat, whereas the company's 13 ton lorry, purchased in 1932, was able to make two round trips to the port in a day.

It is hardly surprising, then, that trade had all but evaporated from the Montgomery Canal well before the fateful breach of 1936. But in the next two or three miles of canal you come upon the remains of some of the key industries which made it successful for a time at least. The wharf at Bridge 82 was linked by tramway to a number of collieries up on Sweeney Mountain, whilst at Crickheath Wharf another tramway connected with quarries at Llynclys and Whitehaven. At the beginning of 2006 funds were being made available to restore the canal onwards to Crickheath Wharf.

Pant was the scene of more interaction between water and rail. The standard gauge Cambrian Railways squeezed through the gap between the canal and the hillside and a station perched over the waterway by Bridge 88. Narrow gauge mineral lines came swooping down from the hillside quarries - hence the extra arch on the offside of the bridge. By Bridge 91 there is a bank of well preserved limekilns.

Summary of Facilities
NAVIGATION INN - canalside Bridge 79. Tel: 01691 672958. Bistro, restaurant and bar rolled into one; accommodation as well in this now stylishly appointed former boatmen's hostelry. At PANT there's a well-stocked Post Office stores and a good pub called the CROSS GUNS (Tel: 01691 830821) up on the A483 along which buses connect with Welshpool and Oswestry - Tel: 0870 608 2 608.

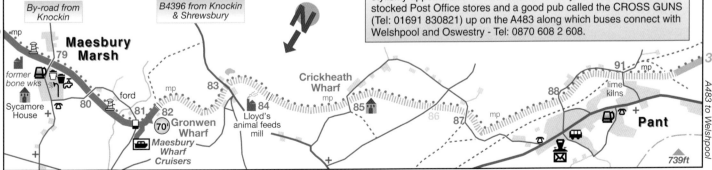

Lime Kilns at Pant

T HE canal skirts the foot of the limestone eminence of Llanymynech Hill. Probably worked for its mineral deposits as long ago as the Iron Age, it now has a golf course on its summit. At the point where a former railway (known as 'Rock Siding') crossed the canal, it comes back into water. A high chimney heralds the approach to the hill's eponymous village, and the indents of old wharves eat into the offside bank. The chimney was the flue for a Hoffman kiln used for the continuous burning of limestone. If you have ever travelled on the Settle & Carlisle railway you'll have passed a similar installation north of Settle.

British Waterways are developing an operations centre in former stabling beside Bridge 92 which, incidentally, marks the frontier between England and Wales.

Bridge 93 is still intact in its hump-backed innocence, but the by-road to Tanat which crossed it has been directed across the bed of the canal. A few hundred yards to the west the canal joins a road to cross the trackbed of the old branchline railway to Llanfyllin. Carreghofa, a typical GWR halt, lay on the other side of the road, deep in a cutting. When the railway was built a temporary aqueduct was constructed pending completion of the permanent one so as not to interrupt canal traffic, and its abandoned arms are still to be seen disappearing into the undergrowth. A similar phenomenon occurs at Bloxwich on the Wyrley & Essington Canal.

Carreghofa Locks are arguably the prettiest on the canal. They are certainly

continued on page 64

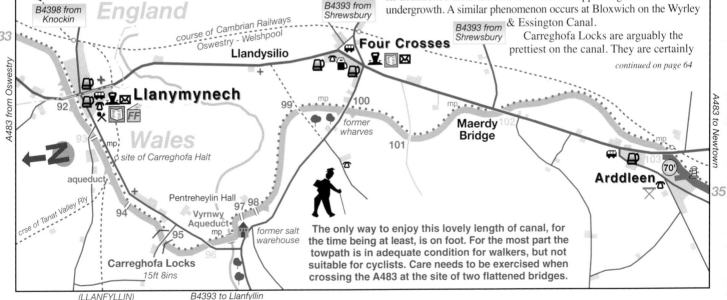

The only way to enjoy this lovely length of canal, for the time being at least, is on foot. For the most part the towpath is in adequate condition for walkers, but not suitable for cyclists. Care needs to be exercised when crossing the A483 at the site of two flattened bridges.

continued from page 63

set on the prettiest section of the entire waterway, amidst gentle wooded hills that epitomise the quiet beauty of Mid Wales. The locks mark the original junction between the Llanymynech Branch of the Ellesmere Canal and the Eastern Branch of the Montgomeryshire Canal. The canalscape here is gorgeous. Look out for the wharfinger's office; the lockhouse with its modest two-storey road frontage masking an altogether more imposing rear; the former side pond between the locks; and the first encounter, for westbound travellers, with the Montgomeryshire Canal's unusual segmented paddle gear. Restored by Shropshire Union Canal Society volunteers, the locks remain unused, for the moment. Another interesting item is an LMS Railway trespass warning sign which overlooks the lower chamber - an authentic survival or post-restoration ornamentation?

An embankment with flood arches, bisected by another flattened road, leads to Vyrnwy Aqueduct, the canal's major engineering structure. Built to the design of John Dadford in 1796, it owes more to the Brindley school of aqueduct construction than Dadford's contemporary, Telford. One of its arches collapsed soon after its opening and, in 1823, George Buck - later to build the magnificent railway viaduct at Stockport - was brought in to strengthen it. Just when he thought he had finished, the walls of the aqueduct bulged and appeared to be collapsing. Buck is said to have smote the ground in despair, but with the help of additional iron tie bars - still prominent to this day - the aqueduct has more or less stood its ground ever since. Cogitate upon this colourful past as you lean upon the parapet of the present and watch the waters of the Vyrnwy glide below. For a more embracing view of the aqueduct, stroll down to the adjacent road bridge from 'bridge' 96.

A dog-leg bend takes the canal off the aqueduct past a refurbished salt warehouse built to last from local stone. Bridge 98, which carried the carriage road to Pentreheylin Hall, has some ornate woodwork. Arcing round the attractive hillside of Bryn Mawr, the canal reaches Four Crosses where there were separate wharves and winding holes either side of Bridge 100.

The approach road to Rhysnant Hall, hidden to the west by folds in the hills, is carried over the canal by Bridge 101. Twice in the next three miles the A483 slices across the bed of the canal, presenting a huge obstacle to restoration.

Llanymynech

Road traffic holds this former quarrying village hostage, bludgeoning the bucolic sensibilities of canal travellers poking their heads up the steps of Bridge 92. Walk down one side of the main street and you are in England, cross the road and you are in Wales. In common with all these border communities, the locals come over as a blurred mixture of Celt and Anglo Saxon; presumably the result of all that illicit inter-marrying down the ages. Speaking of progeny, the village's most famous native is Richard Roberts, inventor of the gasometer. Railway enthusiasts may recognise Llanymynech as the western terminus of the Shropshire & Montgomeryshire Railway, one of Colonel Stephens' impecunious outfits beloved of L. T. C. Rolt, who once propelled a platelayer's trolley from Kinnerley to Llanymynech and back in the same time scheduled for the trains; a statistic which says more about the generosity of the timetable than Rolt's athletic prowess.

Three pubs, a chinese takeaway (Tel: 01691 830426) and an Indian restaurant called BENGAL SPICES (Tel: 01691 830170) provide the canal traveller with a degree of choice. Accommodation for leg-weary towpath walkers is provided by the Les Routiers recommended BRADFORD ARMS - Tel: 01691 830582.

ASHFIELD STORES - Tel: 01691 830770. Well-stocked Post Office stores.

BUSES - Arriva Midland services to/from Oswestry and Welshpool. Useful for towpath walkers. Tel: 0870 608 2 608.

Four Crosses

Reached from Bridge 100, this busy intersection of roads offers a useful range of facilities including: THE FOUR CROSSES (Tel: 01691 831643) and the GOLDEN LION where accommodation is available - Tel: 01691 830295. A well stocked SPAR shop (Tel: 01691 831261) stays open until 10pm daily, and buses run as per Llanymynech.

Arddleen

This roadside village (whose name means 'flax-garden') currently marks the end of navigation north of Welshpool. There is no shop but THE HORSESHOE (Tel: 01938 590318) is a pleasant pub offering bed & breakfast. Buses run as per Llanymynech.

BURGEDIN Locks were reopened in the summer of 1998. Above the locks, where a reedy backwater is all that remains of the Guilsfield Arm, you can only navigate for a mile or so to the flattened A483 bridge at Arddleen, but southwards some eleven miles of navigable canal stretch entertainingly as far as Bridge 129 beyond Berriew. The locks drop the canal by sixteen and a half feet to the sump level of the canal, making the Montgomery a peculiarity in a world where most man-made navigations climb up to, and descend from, a central summit.

At The Wern there is a slipway, winding hole and picnic area; the latter on the site of a former corn mill which derived its power from the sump level's plentiful supply of excess water produced by boats using the locks in either direction.

Southwards from The Wern the canal rides along an embankment above marshy ground, a remnant of the swamp which surrounded the Severn before it was drained early in the 19th century. On the far side of the river stand the Breidden Hills, seldom out of sight since you left Frankton. Now you can enjoy them in detail: quarry-scarred

Breidden Hill itself, the most northerly summit, topped by a monument to Admiral Rodney by way of thanks for using Montgomeryshire timber in the building of his navy; and Moel y Golfa to the south with a memorial to Ernest Burton, King of Romanys. In the foreground are the mysterious masts of Criggion Radio Station, a clandestine establishment rumoured to be used as a tracking station for nuclear submarines.

Bank Lock is the first (or last) of four in close proximity which raise (or lower) the canal by some 35 feet. Each chamber has its segmented ground paddles, though these are not in general use. Crowther Hall Lock is, at 9ft 2ins, the deepest on the canal. The lock cottage has been made habitable once more. Down the adjoining lane is Crowther Hall, a handsome half-timbered farmhouse. Pool Quay's delightful Victorian church, with its notable timber belfry, overlooks the next pound.

continued on page 66

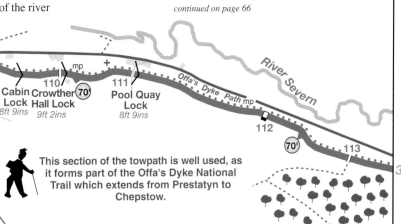

This section of the towpath is well used, as it forms part of the Offa's Dyke National Trail which extends from Prestatyn to Chepstow.

65

continued from page 65

Pool Quay marked the head of navigation on the River Severn. It was, as the name suggests, the port, or quay, for Poole, an earlier name for Welshpool; though previously the settlement, the site of a notable Cistercian monastery, was known as Strata Marcella. The monks brought industry to the banks of the Severn and harnessed the river's power to drive a flour mill, textile works and forge. The Severn could only be navigated this far upstream in winter when there was sufficient depth of water, and with the advent of canal and railway transportation, carrying on the river had ceased by the mid 19th century.

South of Pool Quay, Long Mountain assumes the vertical mantle of the Breiddens. Deep in its trench - unless sufficient rain has fallen on the hills of mid-Wales to make it break its banks - the Severn snakes about its valley floor, a modest watercourse difficult to associate with the broad navigable river of Gloucestershire featured in our *Severn & Avon Companion*. Briefly eluding the A483, the canal hides under the protective, wooded skirts of Yr Allt - a delightful stretch of waterway.

Buttington Wharf

BUTTINGTON Wharf was an early development under the Montgomery Canal restoration programme and was home to the *Heulwen Sunshine*, a specially built trip boat for the handicapped which pioneered navigation on this length of canal from 1976. The wharf, popular with local people, has picnic tables and a trio of preserved limekilns, burnt lime having been widely used as an agricultural fertilizer before the introduction of chemicals. *Heulwen-Sunshine*, and her later sister vessel *Heulwen II*, now have a new base however, at the recently constructed wharf by Bridge 116.

Road schemes seldom benefit canals. You only have to look as far as the Montgomery's flattened bridges to see the truth of this. Yet, paradoxically, the Welshpool by-pass twice came to the rescue of the town's canal: initially in 1969 when it was proposed to route the new road along the bed of the long moribund waterway, the threat of its loss crystallising a latent enthusiasm for the canal; then again in 1992/3 when the by-pass was finally constructed along a different course, allowing the previously flattened Gallows Tree Bank Bridge to be rebuilt with headroom for boats. Final completion of the by-pass and subsequent rebuilding of

Whitehouse Bridge (No 120) has resulted in the release of eleven miles of navigable waterway.

Bungalows with neat gardens and Victorian villas - one with a monkey puzzle tree and a gazebo - herald the approach to Welshpool. Officially opened by Prince Charles in 1983, Welshpool Wharf is located south of Bridge 118 and incorporates a large mooring basin and slipway. Relatively little used at present, it is expected to be a valuable amenity when Montgomery Canal trade 'takes off'. The next (un-numbered) bridge, a metal girder structure, once carried the celebrated Welshpool & Llanfair Light Railway across the canal to its transhipment sidings by the standard gauge Cambrian Railways station, a flamboyant 'French chateau' style building now restored and open as a shopping complex. Eight miles of the 2ft 6ins gauge line pass through delightful countryside from Welshpool's Raven Square station to the rural terminus of Llanfair Caereinion.

Immediately south of the old railway bridge a small aqueduct, dated 1836, carries the canal over Lledan Brook. The semi-circular weir was part of a scheme whereby water was extracted by a local mill.

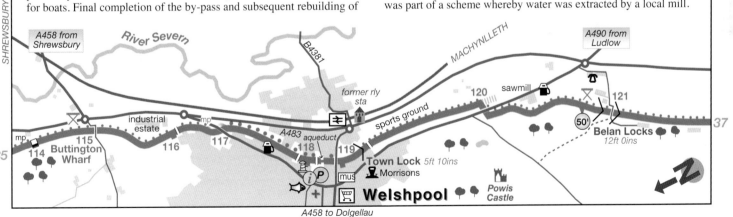

Welshpool's canalscape is quite delightful, the heart being centred on the old canal yard with its imposing and photogenic warehouse and adjoining cottages. The warehouse now serves as a local museum whilst the V shaped basin is used by trip and hire boat operations. Archive photographs reveal that the overflow from Town Lock provided power for the water wheel of an adjoining corn mill.

Beyond the lock, the canal effects its exit from Welshpool rapidly, the urban environs being exchanged for sports grounds, housing and, before long, the gracious landscape of Powis Castle's parkland. A right angled turn takes the canal under Bridge 120 - no longer a barrier to navigation - and along a short new section of canal, wide and deep compared to the original course which is still in water and well utilised for fishing.

Belan Locks soon follow, raising the level of the canal by a total of twelve feet. Close by the lock cottage, with its neatly kept garden, is a group of amazingly ornate black and white cottages, occupied in bygone days by agricultural workers. On the horizon the green hills of Mid Wales enticingly beckon the southbound traveller onwards. But pause for a moment, turn and enjoy again the most splendid view of the Breidden Hills. Sometimes, it seems, the landscape - like life itself - is even better when looking back.

Welshpool (Y Trallwng)

Monday is the day to visit Welshpool when, as well as the general market, the weekly sheep market makes its colourful presence felt in the Smithfield alongside the canal. Down from the hills, farming folk congregate in the town to buy and sell, and to assuage the loneliness of their isolated lives in the freemasonry of the auction ring. And all day the town's pubs hum to the sing-song accents of Mid Wales, whilst the steeply climbing High Street, relatively quiet on other days, reverberates to the passage of cattle lorries, Landrovers and battered old cars plastered in the mud and slurry of far-flung farms.

ROYAL OAK HOTEL - Severn Street. Tel: 01938 552217. Imposing 'Best Western' hotel offering bar and restaurant food for non-residents. Local Welsh beers usually on tap.

THE BUTTERY - High Street. Tel: 01938 552658. Homely half-timbered cafe/restaurant.

OLD STATION RESTAURANT - Old Station. Tel: 01938 556622. Get there before the coach parties!

ANDREWS - High Street. Tel: 01938 552635. Award-winning fish & chips.

Good facilities for a relatively small town reflect Welshpool's importance as a centre for a wide agricultural hinterland. Woolworth's, W.H.Smith, Kwik Save, Somerfield and Boots represent the chain stores, but there are plenty of local retailers too, such as LANGFORD'S the butchers on Berriew Street who specialise in Welsh lamb. There's a useful launderette at the foot of High Street. MORRISONS supermarket alongside Town Lock.

TOURIST INFORMATION CENTRE - Vicarage Garden Car Park (adjoining Bridge 118). Tel: 01938 552043.

POWYSLAND MUSEUM - Local history in the restored canal warehouse. Admission charge. Opening times vary according to season. Tel: 01938 554656.

THE OLD STATION - Severn Road. Tel: 01938 556622. Conglomerate of specialist outlets housed in handsome former station building. Lots to keep the distaff side happy while the male of the species enjoys train sounds and railwayana.

POWIS CASTLE, MUSEUM & GARDEN - World famous garden, medieval castle and Clive Museum displaying treasures from India including textiles, armour, bronzes, jade, ivory etc. National Trust shop and licensed tea room. Admission charge. Open daily April to end of October except Tuesdays and Wednesdays. Tel: 01938 551929.

WELSHPOOL & LLANFAIR RAILWAY - One of the 'Great Little Trains of Wales'. Services operate weekends April to late September, plus half term weekends in October; daily during summer. Tea room at the station at Llanfair, as well as a shop selling a selection of railway books and videos. Tel: 01938 810441.

FLASH LEISURE CENTRE - Salop Road, just up the road from Bridge 117. Visitors made especially welcome. Facilities include swimming pool, sauna, gymnasium, cafe. Tel: 01938 555952.

BUSES - services to/from Shrewsbury, Oswestry and Mid Wales. Tel: 0870 608 2 608.

TRAINS - services to/from Shrewsbury, Newtown and the Cambrian Coast. Tel: 08457 484950.

POWYSLAND MUSEUM AND MONTGOMERY CANAL CENTRE

Welshpool Town Wharf

69

CALLOW Hill, at 1,247 feet, dominates the skyline to the south-east, part of the wonderful Shropshire hill country in the vicinity of Bishop's Castle. Brithdir Lock occupies a most delightful setting, its by-pass weir forming a pond-like feature beside a well-kept lawn. A copse of oak, ash and copper beech trees, set on an almost perfectly-rounded hill, provides an exquisite backdrop.

After climbing almost eight and a half feet through Berriew Lock, the canal is carried on an embankment across the Rhiw Valley and on to Berriew Aqueduct. An 1889 rebuild in brick of an earlier stone structure, the four-arched aqueduct (two river and two land arches) takes the waterway over the fast flowing waters of the Rhiw and the minor road into Berriew.

Flattened Bridge 129, carrying the B4385 road to Berriew, brings to an end the eleven mile navigable section down from Burgedin Locks. Financial constraints meant that construction of the Montgomeryshire Canal stalled in 1797 and for over twenty years Garthmyl, just over 16 miles from Carreghofa, was its terminus. What came to be known as the Western Branch through to Newtown was not completed until 1821. At Garthmyl was concentrated a series of wharves, warehouses, maltings, coal yards, stables and limekilns, and in its heyday the village must have been the scene of intense activity. It still is, but only from cars and lorries thundering along the A483, the widening of which in the 1940s obliterated most of the wharf area, although the old maltings are still in evidence beside an infilled section of canal. Garthmyl is also notable in that it is the closest point on the canal to Montgomery - just three miles away along the B4385. The county town was never an important commercial centre, however, and generated little trade for the canal.

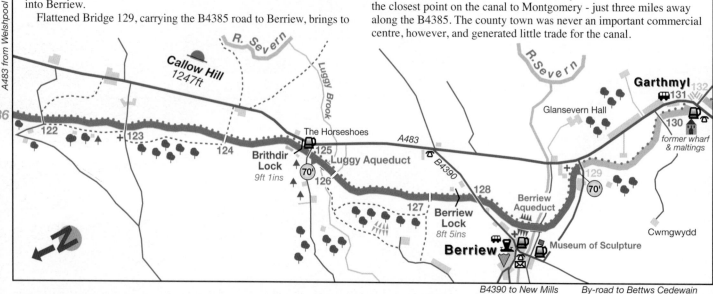

Berriew

Enchanting village beside the River Rhiw, with clusters of black and white cottages huddling around the church and a handsome 18th century single span stone bridge. Good walking country.

THE HORSESHOES - on A483 by Bridge 125. Tel: 01686 640282. Comfortable country pub with garden and good choice of food.

LION HOTEL - village centre. Les Routiers recommended inn offering accommodation, restaurant and bar meals. Tel: 01686 640452.

THE TALBOT - idyllically located beside the River Rhiw. Tel: 01686 640881.

Spar supermarket, post office stores, butchers and gift shop.

SILVER SCENES - silver plated giftware, showroom and factory outlet. Small charge for factory tours. Tel: 01686 640695.

ANDREW LOGAN MUSEUM OF SCULPTURE - beside the river. Tel: 01686 640689. A 'glittering, sparkling, fantasy wonderland' founded by the originator of the Alternative Miss World contest. Shop selling jewellery and sculpture. Cafe.

GLANSEVERN HALL - 18 acres of garden in grounds of Greek Revival house on banks of the Severn. Open May-Sep, Fri, Sat & Bank Hol Mon afternoons. Tel: 01686 640200.

BUSES - services to Shrewsbury, Welshpool and Newtown. Tel: 0870 608 2 608.

Garthmyl

Innocuous hamlet a couple of miles north-west of the old county town of Montgomery. On the bus route and host to a well-appointed country pub called the NAG'S HEAD - Tel: 01686 640287 - which offers food, accommodation and nearby Bishops Castle brewed Six Bells ales.

Belan Chapel

71

BACK in water, surprisingly deep and clear, the Monty meanders contentedly along the Severn Valley, the river and the A483 its constant companions: 'the towpath, in default of one along the Severn, is the pleasantest and easiest walk along the valley' wrote Brian Waters, the poet and topographical writer in *Severn Stream* published in 1949, and half a century has happily done nothing to make one argue with his view.

Two more flattened bridges, either side of the roadside hamlet of Fron, provide a stark reminder of the difficulties facing return of navigable status. William Pugh, one of the prime movers in the canal's extension westwards, was born at Pennant. Wealthy, educated, and philanthropic, he built the Flannel Exchange in Newtown and put so much money into the canal and the local economy that he was forced to flee across the Channel to escape his creditors, dying a pauper's exile in 1842. The creditors may have been confounded, but retrospectively we can thank Pugh for this ravishing canal.

At Brynderwen Lock the towpath briefly changes sides to accommodate

a former coal wharf.

Between Brynderwen and Byles locks, the A483 crosses the canal again before finally moving to the other side of the valley in the vicinity of Abermule; thereafter the canal is left in peace for the remainder of the journey to Newtown. Abermule - a useful staging post for walkers with two pubs, a well-stocked Post Office stores, and regular bus service linking it with Newtown and Welshpool - is perhaps best known for being the site of a major rail disaster in 1921 when two trains - an Aberystwyth-Manchester express and a Whitchurch-Aberystwyth stopping train - collided head on along a stretch of single track; 17 people were killed and 36 injured. A happier railway memory is of the branchline from Abermule which threaded the gorge of the River Mule to the famous sheep-rearing centre of Kerry. Closed in 1956, in its final days the cattle trains, hauled by ancient 'Dean Goods', struggled up the grass-grown line only to serve the monthly sheep fairs.

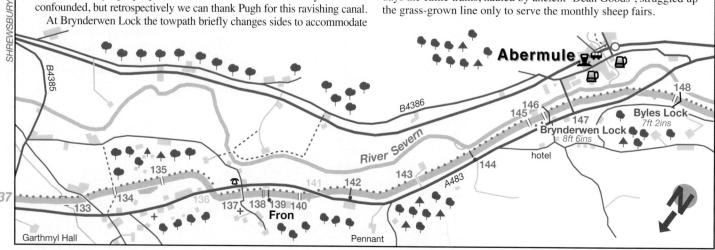

72

DISTURBED only by the occasional walker, the canal below Newhouse Lock is the idyllic haunt of moorhens, coots, kingfishers and dragonflies. Bechan Brook is crossed on a three arched aqueduct before Bridge 152 carries the B4389 road into the hamlet of Aberbechan, the last settlement before Newtown.

Above Freestone Lock - derelict and gateless - the canal bed is dry. At this point the River Severn broadens and a large weir is visible, and audible, from the towpath, its foaming waters seeming to tease the moribund canal's inactivity.

Beyond Dolfor Lock, alongside which stands a large sewage works, the canal bed is no longer discernible, but the waterway may be followed along a good pathway. Whether boats will ever pass this way again remains to be seen, but for the time being it is enjoyable enough to be able to proceed on foot towards Newtown. However, the only significant remains along this section are of the pumping house which drew water for the canal up from the River Severn.

Interestingly, the Montgomery Canal's terminal basin was not, in fact, in old Newtown, the land on the north side of the River Severn being in the separate parish of Llanllwchaiarn. The site is today occupied by a housing estate, which represents something of an anti-climax at the end of the thirty-five mile journey from Welsh Frankton; and a far cry from the heady days of the last century when the area was a veritable hive of industry, around the basin being concentrated numerous limekilns, foundries, coal and timber wharves.

By the twentieth century Newtown's mills were mainly mechanised and, whilst some used water power, others were steam operated and received their coal by canal. The last to do so were the Commercial Mills of Jones, Evans & Co, manufacturers of blankets, shawls and knitted goods. When they closed in 1935, they were still using 20 tons of coal a week. Mined in the collieries at Chirk, it was delivered by Tom Moody in his narrow boat *Endeavour*. Bearing in mind the ever deteriorating state of the Montgomery Canal, the round trip from Chirk probably took around a week to complete and it is doubtful whether he was able to carry any other traffic. When Jones, Evans & Co closed in 1935, Tom Moody stopped work, leaving George Beck as the last surviving boatman on the canal, until the breach of the following year put him out of business too.

for facilities see page 74

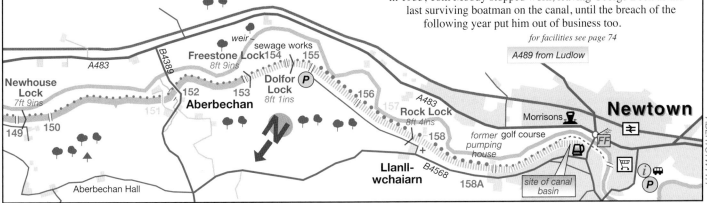

Newtown

A lively and historic town belying its name, and one which will become a worthy terminus of a fully restored Montgomery Canal. Edward I granted the town a charter in 1279 but it was not until the nineteenth century that Newtown grew significantly with development of the woollen industry - at its zenith it was known as the 'Leeds of Wales'. Today it is the major centre for light industry in Mid Wales. Newtown's most famous son was Robert Owen (1771-1858), the successful capitalist whose socialist ideals inspired the Co-operative movement - his statue stands in Shortbridge Street.

WAGGON & HORSES - pub overlooking site of canal terminus. Tel: 01686 625790.

BANK COTTAGE TEA ROOMS - Shortbridge Street. Tel: 01686 625771. Everything a tea room should be!

JARMAN'S FISH RESTAURANT - High Street. Filling fish suppers for hungry walkers. Tel: 01686 625505.

All the major chain stores in the Bear Lanes Precinct off High Street and the Ladywell Shopping Centre off Shortbridge Street. Outdoor market every Tuesday; indoor market (Market Hall, High Street) on Tuesday, Friday and Saturday. Large MORRISONS on A483. Potentially useful launderette on Severn Street.

TOURIST INFORMATION CENTRE - Central Car Park. Tel: 01686 625580.

ROBERT OWEN MUSEUM - The Cross, Broad Street. Museum telling the remarkable story of the man who inspired the Co-operative movement. Admission free. Open Mon-Sat throughout the year. Tel: 01686 626345.

W. H. SMITH MUSEUM - High Street. The shop has been restored to its original state at the time it was first opened in 1927 and on the first floor is a fascinating small museum, highlighting many aspects of the company's business and tradition easily overlooked. Admission free. Open shop hours. Tel: 01686 626280.

TEXTILE MUSEUM - Commercial Street. On north bank of the Severn, enquire locally as to seasonal opening times.

BUSES - Arriva Cymru services to/from Welshpool and Shrewsbury with useful stops at Abermule and Berriew for shorter towpath walks. Tel: 0870 608 2 608.

TRAINS - services to/from Welshpool, Shrewsbury and the Mid-Wales coast. Tel: 08457 484950.

Journey's End

T HE Monmouthshire Canal and the Brecon & Abergavenny Canal were built as two separate waterways. The former, opened in 1799, ran for eleven miles from the Usk Estuary at Newport to Pontnewynydd, north-west of Pontypool, with an eleven mile branch from Malpas to Crumlin; the latter, opened throughout in 1812, linked Brecon with Pontymoile, junction with the Monmouthshire, a distance of some 33 miles. In 1865 the Brecon & Abergavenny Canal was bought by the Monmouthshire Company, with the joint concern being taken over by the Great Western Railway in 1880. Commercial trade ended in the 1930s and the Monmouthshire Canal was largely abandoned, but the Brecon & Abergavenny Canal survived, primarily as a water feeder. With financial support from Monmouthshire and Brecon County Councils, the waterway was restored for navigation by British Waterways and reopened between Brecon and Pontymoile in 1970.

Subsequent restoration work has seen the limit of navigation pushed south as far as Five Locks, Cwmbran. Further proposals exist to restore the Mon & Brec all the way down to Newport and thus provide a link with the rest of the inland waterway network by way of the Usk and Severn estuaries. But for the time being navigability begins, or ends, at Five Locks, Cwmbran, where a lowered road bridge and a flight of five derelict locks bar any further progress south. A mooring basin and winding point have been provided and the surroundings are pleasant, if suburban, and a charming wooden sculpture of a narrowboat graces the presently infilled chamber of the top lock.

Inky and weedy and pea soup green with algae, the canal water betrays a prevalent hesitancy amongst boaters to venture south of Pontymoile. True, some may find the post-industrial communities of Pontnewydd, Sebastopol and Griffithstown too dour for their holiday-making sensibilities, but this is the *real* South Wales, an urban landscape of terraced houses and telegraph poles and time standing, appar-

By-road from Upper Cwmbran

golf course

tunnel

course of Monmouthshire Canal

A 472 from Pontypool

Cwmbran

Pontnewydd

Sebastopol

46

47   48

rse of Newport - Blaenavon rly

former steelworks

Open Hearth

Griffithstown

Narrows   50

49

Railway Museum

hosp.

51

McDonalds

Pontypool Park

Pontymoile Basin

52   slipway
aqueduct

wc

53

The Folly Tower

low pipe

55   56

54   55'

New Inn

Pontypool & New Inn

Horse & Jockey

57   58

65'

41

A4042 to Newport

HEREFORD   A4042 to Abergavenny

ently if not statistically, still. There is much to look out for and enjoy: Cwmbran Tunnel - just 87 yards long with a path over the top - lies cradled in a little bower of green open space separating Pontnewydd from Sebastapol and by its northern portal a surviving Monmouthshire Canal milepost informs that the Newport terminus of the canal lies 7 miles to the south; the trackbed of the Newport & Pontypool Railway crosses the canal on high, skewed girders by Bridge 51, and nearby a museum celebrates (amongst myriad other railway matters) that the Associated Society of Locomotive Engineers and Firemen was formed here in 1880; the rather forbidding hospital bordering the offside of the canal between bridges 50 and 51, originally the Pontypool Poor Law Institution.

Pontymoile Basin marks the former junction of the Monmouthshire and Brecon & Abergavenny canals. Nowadays it's a popular leisure asset for nearby Pontypool. A tearoom and picnic site draw the locals, whilst the old toll house is available for holiday lets - Tel: 0800 542 2663. Here, in the canal's working past, boats were assessed for tolls as they went from one canal to the other. Close by, an aqueduct - the tallest on the Mon & Brec - carries the canal over the Afon Llwyd.

Summary of Facilities

OPEN HEARTH - canalside between bridges 48 & 49. Tel: 01495 763752. A tradition of steel-making gives this friendly canalside pub its curious name. Nine real ales to choose from and a wide-ranging menu make this arguably the best port of call in the vicinity of Sebastopol and Griffithstown.
HORSE & JOCKEY - east of Bridge 55. Tel: 01495 762721. Pretty thatched pub within easy reach of the canal. Good food and Greene King portfolio ales. Nice garden.
Also: fish & chips by Bridge 48, and a McDonalds drive-thru and Harvester restaurant overlooking the roundabout east of Pontymoile Basin once occupied by 86G - Pontypool Road railway engine shed!

It's preferable that you lay on stores higher up the canal, for along this lower navigable length one has to rely on the meagre stocks of corner shops for victualling the galley.
GRIFFITHSTOWN RAILWAY MUSEUM - Station Road, Griffithstown (east of Bridge 49). Tel: 01495 762908. Former Great Western Railway goods shed housing a nostalgic collection of railwayana recalling the great days of 'God's Wonderful Railway' generally, and the dense railway network of the local area specifically. Also celebrates Charles Perry, founder of ASLEF. Open daily, small admission fee, refreshments.

TRAINS - stations at Cwmbran and Pontypool & New Inn offer links with the outside world and the possibility of one-way towpath walks to/from Abergavenny. Tel: 08457 484950.

Backyards, Griffithstown

OUTPOSTS of industry - fibre and pharmaceutical plants - pepper the valley, but up in its hillside setting, the canal remains tree-lined and secretive, demarcating the boundaries of traditional hill farms, like the picturesquely whitewashed one between bridges 75 and 76 with the monkey puzzle tree in its small garden. Look out also for the peculiar house by Bridge 81 with an opening for a boat at water level. GOYTRE WHARF is one of the canal's showpieces, a well-preserved example of the kind of industrial facility which flourished in the canal's commercial heyday with arms and a rank of limekilns. Goytre Wharf Heritage Activity & Study Centre celebrates the role the wharf played in local transport before the advent of the railway - Tel: 01873 881069.

This stretch of the canal features in Alexander Cordell's historical saga *Rape of the Fair Country* in which he writes vividly of lying on the prow of a barge watching the water-lilies and bindweed waving as sunlight streams through the trees casting golden patterns on the boat. Another of his books - widely available locally - called *Song of the Earth* is set on the Neath & Tennant Canals.

WATERSIDE RESTAURANT - cafe/restaurant located at Goytre Wharf adjoining the Canal Centre. Tel: 01873 881355. HORSESHOE INN - quarter of a mile north of Bridge 65. Another comfortable country inn also offering accommodation for those preferring to explore the canal on foot. Tel: 01873 880542.

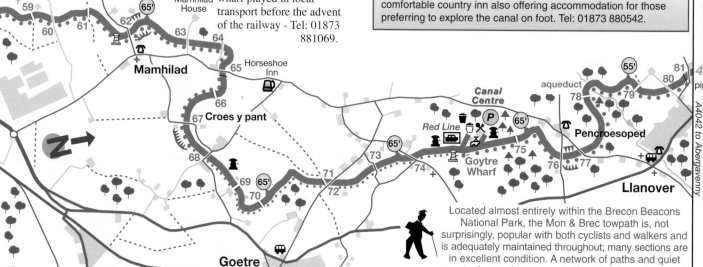

Located almost entirely within the Brecon Beacons National Park, the Mon & Brec towpath is, not surprisingly, popular with both cyclists and walkers and is adequately maintained throughout; many sections are in excellent condition. A network of paths and quiet country lanes give access to the hills above the canal.

Dog-walking near Mamhilad

FREQUENT occupation bridges - some humped, some flat-decked - punctuate the canal's progress along the 367 foot contour line above the valley of the Usk, visually framing successive lengths of water flanked by trees. Occasionally you find yourself wishing, uncharacteristically, that there were less trees, because they do tend to mask the views, so it is tempting to reach for your rucksack and take to the hills to do more justice to such splendid scenery. Between bridges 85 and 87, towpath walkers can shave a few hundred yards off the journey, by taking to a path through the woods. This path runs steeply down to cross a stream on a footbridge bearing a sign warning of the existence of a troll - see what you miss by keeping resolutely to the canal! Llanover House belonged to one Benjamin Hall, who, as Commissioner of Works, gave his name to London's horological landmark, Big Ben.

Llanfoist Wharf is the home of Beacon Park Boats, surely one of the most beautifully-sited hire bases in the country. It may be difficult to imagine that this quiet place was once the scene of intense industrial activity. Hill's tramroad linked the ironworks at Blaenavon and forge at Garnddyrys with the canal wharf and the Llanvihangel tramroad on the valley floor below. There was a substantial marshalling yard of lines at Llanfoist Wharf with the present cottage being the signal box. To explore the route of the tramroad, go down the steps beside Tod's Bridge to reach the road and the entrance to the tunnel, which leads uphill beneath the canal to the tramroad incline. The route can be followed up the hillside and on to the lower slopes of the Blorenge Mountain.

As well as the launch pad for a journey into the past, Llanfoist Wharf represents the canal's closest point to the lively and historic town of Abergavenny, the centre of which lies a country mile away on the east bank of the Usk. You could walk it within half an hour, but a fairly good bus service operates from stops in the village of Llanfoist; just bear in mind

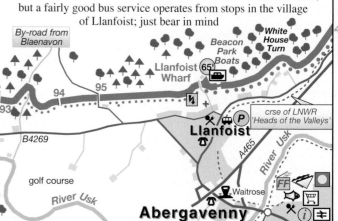

that it's a steep climb back!

The Brecon & Abergavenny Canal, like the Monmouthshire, was built by Thomas Dadford Junior. His design was for a contour canal and the 25 mile pound between Five Locks, Cwmbran and Llangynidr - one of the longest in the country - ranks as a remarkable achievement in such mountainous terrain. The waterway twists and turns in an attempt to maintain the 367 foot contour, at times seeming to cling ever more desperately to the hillside. It hasn't always succeeded in doing so. A number of breaches have occurred, including a major one at White House Turn, Llanfoist, in 1975, when thousands of gallons of water cascaded down onto parts of the village below the canal. Unfortunately, the brunt of the watery assault was borne by a number of fine houses, and an unofficial campaign gathered momentum to have the canal closed at this point. Consequently, it was six long years before British Waterways could overcome local hostility, repair the breach and reopen this section again in 1981.

Llanfoist

The remains of Alexander Cordell, chronicler of 19th century industrial life in the Valleys, lie in the cemetery of the pretty little church of Llanfoist which you pass on your steep descent from the canal. The local pub has been turned into an Asian restaurant since our last visit and the post office stores become seemingly a victim of the supermarket on its doorstep. Regular bus services operate to Abergavenny. Station Cars - Tel: 01873 857233 - provide a more personalised transport link.

Abergavenny

'Markets, Mountains and More' is the present tourist propaganda employed to tempt you into visiting this historic town at the confluence of the Gafenni and Usk rivers. No need, now, to rely on those old enough to remember Marty Wilde's engaging rendition of the eponymous pop ditty *Taking a Trip up to Abergavenny*, which brought him everlasting fame in the locality. Pop trivia aside, Abergavenny is a thoroughly likeable place which you should aim to visit despite lying at arm's length from the canal. A relatively unspoilt tourist centre catering for walkers and other outdoor types, it also serves as a market town for South-East Wales.

ANGEL HOTEL - Cross Street. Tel: 01873 857121. Handsome coaching inn offering bar and restaurant food for non-residents.
THE TRADING POST - Nevill Street. Tel: 01873 855448. Atmospheric coffee house and bistro.
MARKET STREET FISH & CHIPS - Market Street. Classic fish & chips restaurant/take-away. Tel: 01873 855791.
COLISEUM - Lion Street. Wetherspoon conversion of old cinema. Tel: 01873 736960.
LA BRASSERIE - Lewis's Lane. Tel: 01873 737937. Hidden treasure!
WALNUT TREE INN - Llanddewi Skirrid. Tel: 01873 852797. Internationally famous restaurant three miles from Abergavenny. A taxi jaunt for the well-heeled hungry.

Twenty minutes walk from the canal, there's a WAITROSE supermarket. But it's Abergavenny's independent shops - like Vin Sullivan's delicatessen (Frogmore Street) Rawlings the butchers (Market Street), Wales Fish Company (Frogmore Street) and Edwards butcher and delicatessen on Flannel Street - that really contribute to the pleasure of shopping here. Look out too for the Abergavenny Book Shop on High Street and Abergavenny Music on Cross Street if you're a bookworm or music lover. The lively market which they're so proud of takes place on Tuesday. Don't miss Burton's men's clothes shop retaining its 'Tailor of Taste' slogan and gold-leafed list of towns with branches.

i TOURIST INFORMATION - Swan Meadow, Monmouth Road. Tel: 01873 857588.
ABERGAVENNY MUSEUM AND CASTLE - Castle Street. Admission charge. Open daily March-October, closed Sundays November-February. Displays trace the history of the town from Roman times. Tel: 01873 854282.
LINDA VISTA GARDENS - Tudor Street. Admission free. Lovely garden featuring trees and shrubs from around the world.
SUGAR LOAF MOUNTAIN - Perhaps the finest - and not unduly difficult - walk in the area is to the 1,955ft summit of the Sugar Loaf mountain. The view from the top will stay with you for ever! Advice on this and other walks from the TIC.

BUSES - services to/from Brecon, Cardiff, Pontypool, Cwmbran and Newport. Cardiff service calls at Llanfoist, Govilon and Gilwern; Brecon buses stop at Crickhowell and Talybont. Tel: 0870 608 2 608.
TRAINS - services to/from Shrewsbury, Pontypool and Newport. Tel: 08457 484950.
TAXIS - Central Cars. Tel: 01873 50197.

GOVILON Wharf plays host to British Waterways Section Office for South Wales & Somerset Canals, as well as to Govilon Boat Club. The wharf was once the terminus of the Llanvihangel tramroad, opened to Llanvihangel in 1814 and to Hereford in 1819. Closed in 1846, it subsequently became a railway, a branch line between Abergavenny and Merthyr. In *The Forgotten Railways of South Wales* (published by David & Charles in 1979) James Page opined this sadly abandoned railway line 'the most spectacular in South Wales'. Its passenger trains had gone by 1958 but the station, just uphill from Bridge 98, has become a private home whilst the trackbed is now a footpath and cycleway. William Bliss alighted here with his canoe and baggage to begin his canoeing trip along the Mon & Brec Canal, as described in *Rapid Rivers*, published in 1935. He wrote of this section of the canal: 'I landed on the right bank and walked across the road, and then saw below me the Usk valley clothed in woods and the town of

Abergavenny on the further side, and opposite to me the Sugar Loaf hill and behind that the great mass of the Black Mountains rising up to nearly three thousand feet. Then the canal made a bend to cross the little Llanwenarth brook, and between that and Gilwern there were wonderful open views from the canal itself up the Usk Valley. I was glad I had come. It was late May, and everything was green and happy and there was no-one there but me'.

Amazingly little has changed. There are still wonderful views up the Usk Valley and across to the Sugar Loaf and Black Mountains, and everything is still 'green and happy'. As for there being 'no-one there', well we can't promise that, but the Mon & Brec is considerably quieter than the main canal network. Like most isolated waterways, it exudes a faint air of superiority, rather like an exclusive club. But just come and walk the towpath, or hire a boat for a spell, and you too can be a

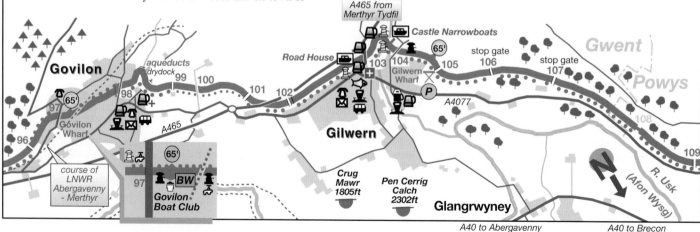

member.

The Heads of the Valleys Road Bridge provides a test of skill for the most accomplished steerer, requiring a ninety degree turn to be executed in a confined space. Then GILWERN makes its presence felt, its housing estates being unwelcome intruders in this magical world of mountains and valleys, woodlands and streams. But this is an important boating centre, within the parameters of this peaceful canal, boasting two hire bases, and a good choice of pubs.

Gilwern is also one of the most important historical sites on the Mon & Brec. Through Gilwern Bridge a right-angled bend at the start of Gilwern Wharf takes the canal across the Clydach Gorge on a 90 foot high embankment. On the south side was the Clydach Iron Company's wharf, where the Llam-march tramroad brought down coal from the Llam-march mines and iron from the Clydach ironworks. Below the canal ran both the river and the Clydach Railroad, which went down to the Usk at Glangrwyney, a mile from Gilwern. Branches led to further wharves and to the Clydach Basin, now the hire base of Castle Narrowboats. Mooring facilities are provided on both sides of the aqueduct and paths and steps link the wharf, towpath and tramroad tunnel, allowing a thorough exploration of the area. The next bridge, No 104, was the site of a number of limekilns and an old coal wharf, originally constructed by the Brecon Boat Company.

Firmly ensconced within the Brecon Beacons National Park, the canal traverses a densely wooded section west of Gilwern. The trees serve to block off views of the Usk Valley, but redeem themselves by shielding the canal from the busy A4077 road which runs alongside for a mile or so.

Govilon

The massive bulk of the Blorenge mountain looms over Govilon dominating the village as the Matterhorn dominates Zermatt. A romanticised analogy perhaps, but Govilon's setting is truly dramatic, especially in winter when the great hill is snow covered. In contrast, the village itself is unremarkable, comprising mainly modern housing.

BRIDGEND INN - via Bridge 98 or the aqueduct. CAMRA recommended pub serving a good choice of guest beers. Lunches, evening meals and a self-evident enthusiasm for folk music. Tel: 01873 830177. Another pub called The Lion down in the village.

Post office stores and gift shop handy to the canal though not quite as much choice as in neighbouring Gilwern.

BUSES - hourly Mon-Sat service provided by Lewis Taxis linking Govilon with Abergavenny and Bryn-mawr. Tel: 0870 608 2 608.

Gilwern

Humdrum village in a wonderful setting - breathtaking views across the Usk Valley to the Black Mountains.

BRIDGEND INN - canalside Bridge 103. Tel: 01873 830939. Felinfoel beers from Llanelli and a good choice of food.

NAVIGATION - canalside Bridge 103. Tel: 01873 830213. Nice waterside garden.

Fish & chips adjacent to Bridge 103 - Tel: 01873 832040 - 'all our cod is freshly cooked'!

Post office, general store and pharmacy on road leading down from Bridge 103; SPAR shop in garage on A4077.

BUSES - Stagecoach service X4 hourly Mon-Sat to/from Abergavenny and Cardiff via Pontypridd. Tel: 0870 608 2 608.

A SPECTACULAR panorama greets the Brecon bound traveller emerging from the woods beyond Bridge 109. Glance behind at the Sugar Loaf; down to Crickhowell nestling beside the Usk against the dramatic backdrop of Table Mountain and the Black Mountains; and ahead to the imposing bulk of Mynydd Llangattock. Remember the passage through Llanfoist Wood and thinking that the scenery couldn't get any better? Perhaps it can after all. Try mooring for the night near Bridge 111, then, as daylight fades, watch the lights twinkling in the cottages and farms far across the valley, like a sea of stars in a cloudless sky. It was on this section, close by Bridge 110, that cutting of the canal began in April 1796.

LLANGATTOCK is the most obvious mooring point for a visit to the pleasant town of Crickhowell, a mile away across the Usk. On the way you cross Crickhowell Bridge which, in its present form, dates from 1810. From downstream it appears to have 13 arches, from upstream 12!

There are limekilns at the wharf beyond Bridge 115; another tramroad route (Darren Cilau) leading up the Llangattock escarpment from Bridge 114; and an aqueduct over the Nant Onneu, a tributary of the Usk. And all around are the magnificent mountains. A stiff two hour climb, partly following the route of the tramroad, will take you to the summit of Mynydd Pen-cyrn (1735 feet).

Bridge 118 is known as Workhouse Bridge, but the object of this haunting association has thankfully become an hospitable hotel called TY CROSESO - Tel: 01873 810573.

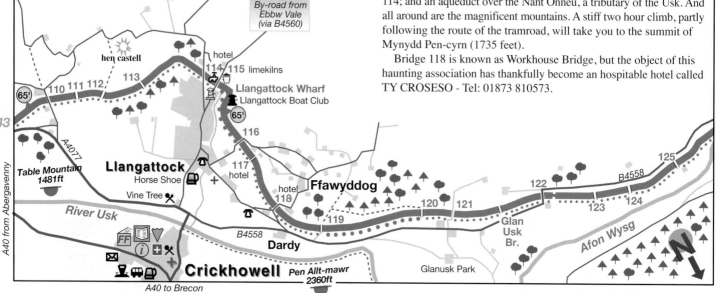

Llangattock

Llangattock takes its name from the church of St Catwg, founded in the 6th century and rebuilt in the 12th. Tucked away down a narrow lane, the village stocks and whipping post are contained within its grounds. Dominated by the quarried face of the Llangattock escarpment, the village is a mix of modern bungalows and old cottages.

HORSE SHOE INN - village centre. Tel: 01873 810393. Bar meals lunchtimes and evenings.
THE VINE TREE - A4077. Nicely appointed bar and restaurant overlooking Crickhowell Bridge, well worth the walk down from the canal. Breconshire Brewery beers. Tel: 01873 810514.

Crickhowell

Small Welsh towns just don't come any more delightful than Crickhowell. The name is the Anglicised form of Crug Hywel, the rampart and the ditch stronghold of Hywel Dda - now known as Table Mountain, which overlooks the town.

BEAR HOTEL - High Street. Tel: 01873 810408. Immensely comfortable and welcoming 15th century coaching inn; all beams, big fireplaces and flagstones. Bar and restaurant meals plus very tempting accommodation. Winner of many awards!

Shopping here is a pleasure. Two small supermarkets and an interesting variety of individual local shops. NatWest and Lloyds TSB have branches in the town.
BACCHUS, the appropriately named off licence, stocks local beers.

TOURIST INFORMATION CENTRE - Beaufort Street. Tel: 01873 812105. (Closed in winter).

BUSES - services to Brecon and Abergavenny. Tel: 0870 608 2 608. TAXIS - 01873 811764.

Old lime kilns, Llangattock

AT Llangynidr (difficult for the English to pronounce but try 'Llan-gun-idder') the 25 mile pound from Five Locks, Cwmbran finally comes to an end. It makes a pleasant change to have some locks to work and, like English wickets going down in a Test Match, you don't just get one or two, but five in quick succession. Designed - like most locks in South Wales - to accommodate boats of 63ft length and 8ft 6ins beam, they are spread over less than a mile and lift the canal up by 48 feet. Local practice is to leave the locks empty with bottom gates open; something of an inconvenience as it means you always have to fill the lock first when locking down, or empty it afterwards when locking up. But no-one should be in a hurry to work through the Llangynidr locks,

as it's difficult to think of a more gorgeous flight anywhere in Britain (perhaps only Bosley on the Macclesfield comes close). Between the first and second locks the canal crosses the River Crawnon on a sizeable aqueduct equipped with a plug and conventional windlass to drain this section of the canal. Public moorings are provided here, presenting the opportunity to be lulled to sleep by the babbling waters of the Crawnon. Above the second lock is the hire base of Country Craft, then the top three locks follow in quick succession, overlooked by the almost perfectly rounded summit of Tor y Foel.

A former workhouse - subsequently two agricultural workers' cottages - stands beside Bridge 136. Today it serves as a highly desirable private residence.

The keen hiker will rapidly realise that a boat on the Mon & Brec can be used as a kind of floating base camp, providing convenient access to many of the loftier summits in the Brecon Beacons National Park. Bridge 134, for example, represents a good starting point for the wonderful ascent of Tor y Foel (1806ft). For a gentler walk from Llangynidr, we can also recommend the path that follows the Usk up and downstream from the B4560 road bridge.

Map labels: Tor y Foel 1806ft · 137 · 138 · 136 · 139 · B4558 · Snake Br. · 135 · 415ft · 140 · Llangynidr Locks 48ft 0ins · 141 · Ashford Tunnel · aqueduct · Brecon Day Boats · 134 · Country Craft · Coach & Horses · 133 · 142 · 65' · B4560 from Ebbw Vale · pipe · Travellers Rest · Red Lion · Llangynidr · P · 132 · 367ft · 131 · 128 · aqueduct · 129 · 130 · 127 · 126 · Gliffaes · B4560 · A40 · A40 to Abergavenny · A40 to Brecon · 44

Lower Lock,
Llangynidr

Ashford Tunnel is 375 yards long with no towpath; in bygone days horses went over the top and boats were poled through. It was built as a 'dig and fill tunnel', whereby a cutting was first made and the tunnel built, then the earth was put back over the tunnel. Boaters need to exercise caution, as it is very narrow with low headroom, particularly towards the Llangynidr end. At the southern portal a plaque commemorates the fact that, after a period of closure for repair, the tunnel was officially reopened on 5th May 1985, the ceremony being performed by Mr Trevor Luckuck; his name is depicted in large capital letters. Mr Luckuck was, of course, British Waterways' Deputy Chief Executive at the time. How could you possibly have forgotten?

Beyond the tunnel the B4558 runs alongside the canal but carries little traffic. Peace and tranquillity still rule the roost hereabouts.

Llanynidr

Set in perhaps the most dramatic section of the Usk Valley, Llangynidr is undoubtedly one of the shiniest jewels in the Mon & Brec crown. The village comprises three distinct parts: Upper Llangynidr, half a mile from Bridge 129; Cwm Crawnon close to the 'Coach & Horses'; and Lower Llangynidr, also known as Coed-yr-Ynys, which is down by the Usk. The latter is the most pleasing, an enchanting jumble of cottages close to the ancient and picturesque six-arched bridge over the river. The locals tell us that when the weather is hot, bathing from the flat rocks in the Usk is an experience not to be missed. Can you believe it's ever that warm? We can't, but we'll settle for enjoying the breathtaking views of the valley from Usk Bridge. Good at any time of the year, but most memorable in late October/early November.

RED LION HOTEL - Upper Llangynidr. Bar & restaurant meals plus bed & breakfast in this nice old inn near the church. Tel: 01874 730223.
COACH & HORSES - canalside Bridge 133. Justifiably one of the most popular pubs on the Mon & Brec. Good choice of beers, bar and restaurant meals, accommodation and attractive canalside garden. Tel: 01874 730245.
WALNUT TREE STORES, in Lower Llandgynidr, is a remarkably well-stocked village stores/newsagent/off licence open until 9.30pm daily. Post office up the road from Bridge 131.
BUSES - occasional services to Brecon and Abergavenny via Crickhowell. Tel: 0870 608 2 608.

Bridge 144 at Talybont on Usk - restricted usage during term-time!

STOP

144

EXECUTING a nifty right angled turn, the Mon & Brec drifts across the Afon Caerfanell on a narrow aqueduct and into Talybont-on-Usk, focal point of the northern end of the canal. It's hardly Skegness or Alton Towers, but the village is the most popular port of call on the waterway, and you may encounter canoeists on the canal, mountain bikers on the towpath and hikers in the hills. Many people arriving here - ourselves included - find it hard to drag themselves away, so much is there to see and do, including exploration of the route of the old Bryn Oer Tramroad, which ran for twelve miles from the Bryn Oer colliery near Rhymney via the Trevil limestone quarry. It forms part of the Taff Trail, a long distance path from Cardiff to Brecon that continues along the towpath to the canal terminus. Running parallel to the tramroad is the line of the former Brecon & Newport Railway, which closed in 1963.

Talybont drawbridge was converted into a fixed structure in 1944,

thus preventing navigation to Brecon to all but canoes and very small boats. It was replaced by a wooden drawbridge in 1970 when the canal was reopened throughout. The present bridge is electrically powered.

A series of lift bridges follows, all hydraulically operated, before the canal passes through the moat of Pencelli Castle. Apart from the original mound, little remains of the once significant medieval castle, although Pencelli Castle farmhouse has taken both its name and some of its stone.

Take a deep breath - the most awe-inspiring section of this fabulous canal is just about to begin. Weather permitting, you'll get your first sight of Pen y Fan, highest of the Brecon Beacons at 2907 feet, a four hour (one way) climb from Bridge 158 via Llanfrynach. Even better views of the Beacons are to come at Bridge 160, beyond the marina and hire base of Cambrian Cruisers. Certainly this canal lives up to E. F. Schumacher's epithet - 'Small is Beautiful'.

For details of facilities at Talybont and Pencelli see page 91.

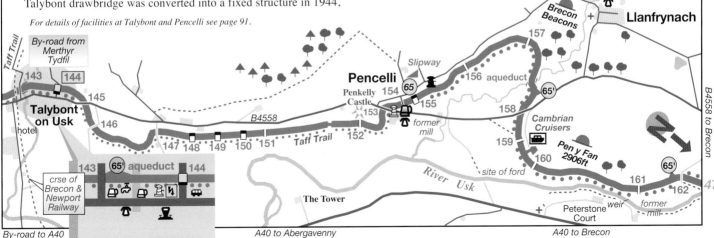

LIKE a championship race horse clearing the final fence at Aintree, the canal leaps powerfully across the River Usk on a substantial four arched stone aqueduct approached (from both directions) by a right angled bend. The water channel narrows to 12 feet for the length of the aqueduct, and at the south end an overflow weir takes away winter flood water. Extensive repairs were carried out on the aqueduct in 1996-97, during which mooring bollards were installed close to the overflow weir. This is a popular overnight stop, although noise from the nearby A40 road detracts slightly from its appeal.

Now there's just the small matter of Brynich ('Best in Wales 2005') Lock to negotiate - lifting the canal up by 10 feet to its summit level of 425 feet - and you're on the final stage of the journey to Brecon. Above the lock the water is deep and crystal clear; it's such a novelty for canal water to be so clean that you tend to stare transfixed over the side of the boat, expecting to see ... who knows what? We saw nothing, except several shoals of silvery fish and several shoals of silvery beer cans. On land the Beacons make their final

appearance for a while, towering imperiously above the lesser hills that surround them.

The towpath here is designated the Brecon to Brynich cycleway; it's very popular with mountain bikers and more serious cyclists. On the offside the B4601 road runs close alongside, but a thick belt of trees prevents traffic noise from becoming intrusive.

Until comparatively recently the canal voyage to Brecon ended with something of a whimper, as the waterway ground to a miserable halt in a wall beyond Gasworks Bridge. Gasworks Bridge! The name conjures up all sorts of images, none of which are appropriate to the Mon & Brec. But now the canal ends, if not with a bang, at least with a sizeable pop, at Theatre Basin - an admirable joint venture funded by Powys Council, the Welsh Arts Council and private enterprise. Passing under a new bridge, named after Thomas Dadford, the canal's engineer, you arrive in the basin which provides extensive moorings as well as a winding point. You can tie up in pleasant surroundings outside the new Brecon Theatre, the perfect place to reflect on your visit to the Monmouthshire & Brecon Canal, a waterway of immense beauty and unique, self-defining charm.

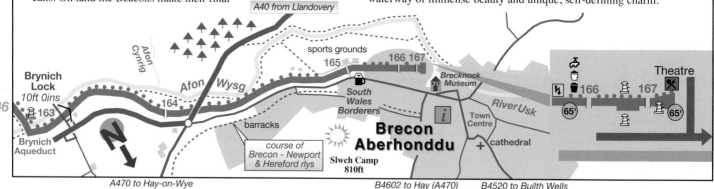

Brecon/Aberhonddu

Market town, administrative centre for the Brecon Beacons National Park, seat of the diocese of Swansea and Brecon and mecca for walkers and climbers, Brecon is a friendly place; certainly no anti-climax at the end of a voyage up the Mon & Brec. The oldest part of town surrounds the castle remains near the confluence of the Usk and Honddu rivers. An attractive 'promenade' by the Usk, reached via Watergate, provides superb views of the Beacons. Every August, New Orleans comes to town with the staging of the internationally-renowned Brecon Jazz Festival.

THE WELLINGTON HOTEL - The Bulwark. Tel: 01874 625225. Town centre hotel offering bar and restaurant food plus an 'authentic' French creperie called Eliza Blues.

ROBERTO'S - St Mary Street. Little Italian restaurant overlooked by St Mary's Church. Tel: 01874 611880.

BRECON BALTI - Glamorgan Street. Tel: 01874 624653. Restaurant and takeaway.

BULL'S HEAD - The Struet. Tel: 01874 622044. Good food, accommodation and a wide choice of real ale.

OLD BOAR'S HEAD - Ship Street. Tel: 01874 622856. Brewery tap for Breconshire Brewery idyllically located by the River Usk.

SARAH SIDDONS - High Street. Tel: 01874 610666. Atmospheric town centre pub offering weekday lunches. Named after the Victorian actress who was born here.

Most of the major stores you'd expect to find in a town of this size, many of them in the new Bethel Square shopping precinct by the main car park. Plenty of outdoor activity shops - a good place to buy that new pair of walking boots. The indoor market dates from 1840 and markets are held on Tuesdays and Fridays with the addition of lively farmer's markets on the second Saturday of each month. MORRISONS supermarket. ANDREW MORTON'S secondhand bookshops on Lion Street and Lion Yard (Tel: 01874 620022 & 620086) are excellent and often seem to stock interesting and rare inland waterways literature.

(i) TOURIST INFORMATION CENTRE - Main Car Park. Tel: 01874 622485.

BRECKNOCK MUSEUM - Captain's Walk. Open daily. Admission charge. Local history, natural history, plus varied exhibitions. Tel: 01874 624121.

BRECON CATHEDRAL - Tel: 01874 625222. Former Benedictine priory refurbished by George Gilbert Scott in 1872. Tithe barn heritage centre and restaurant.

SOUTH WALES BORDERERS AND MONMOUTHSHIRE REGIMENTAL MUSEUM - The Barracks. Open daily Apr-Sept, weekdays Oct-Mar. Admission charge. The history of two famous regiments over 300 years. Tel: 01874 613310.

DRAGONFLY CRUISES - Theatre Basin. Public boat trips from Brecon out to Brynich Lock and back. Tel: 07831 685222.

BIKE HIRE - Bi-Ped Cycles, Free Street. Tel: 01874 622296.

BUSES - alas no 'deep panting' Pannier tanks make their wheezy way up from Newport on the incomparable Brecon & Merthyr line via Torpantau and Pontsticill Junction, nor is there a rail link, as once with Hereford via Hay-on-Wye. In their place buses link Brecon with Crickhowell, Abergavenny and intermediate villages. Also to Hay-on-Wye, Hereford and Merthyr. Tel: 0870 608 2 608.

TAXIS - A & A Cabs Tel: 01874 622288.

Talybont-on-Usk (Map 46)

Quiet holiday centre that relishes its position beside, or rather, below the canal which passes through the village on a substantial embankment. Visitors include cavers, abseilers and rock climbers as well as boaters.

Four inns cater for most tastes and all offer both food and accommodation. They are: TRAVELLER'S REST - adjacent Bridge 142 (Map 45). Tel: 01874 676233. WHITE HART - Bridge 143. Tel: 01874 676227. STAR INN - canalside by aqueduct. Tel: 01874 676635. Best choice of beer! USK INN - Tel: 01874 676251.

Well stocked post office stores also offering hot & cold snacks and carry-out teas and coffees for towpath walkers and others in need of sustenance.

BUSES -to/from Abergavenny and Brecon. Tel: 0870 608 2 608.

Pencelli (Map 46)

Shopless village on the B4558, but there is a snug little pub called the ROYAL OAK, a 300 year old inn featuring home-made food, canalside garden and a choice of locally-brewed real ales. Tel: 01874 665396

Hire Bases

ALVECHURCH BOAT CENTRES - Wrenbury Mill, Llangollen Canal, Map 19. Anderton, Trent & Mersey Canal, Map 31. Tel: 0121 445 2909. www.alvechurch.com

ANDERSEN BOATS - Middlewich, Trent & Mersey Canal, Map 29. Tel: 01606 833668. www.andersenboats.com

ANGLO WELSH - Bunbury, Shropshire Union Canal, Map 13. Trevor, Llangollen Canal, Map 26. Tel: 0117 304 1122. www.anglowelsh.co.uk

BEACON PARK BOATS - Llanfoist, Monmouthshire & Brecon Canal, Map 42. Tel: 01873 858277. www.beaconparkboats.com

BLACK PRINCE NARROWBOATS - Chirk, Llangollen Canal, Map 25. Tel: 01527 575115. www.black-prince.com

CAMBRIAN CRUISERS - Pencelli, Monmouthshire & Brecon Canal, Map 46. Tel: 01874 665315. www.cambriancruisers.com

CASTLE NARROWBOATS - Gilwern, Monmouthshire & Brecon Canal, Map 43. Tel: 01873 830001. www.castlenarrowboats.co.uk

COUNTRY CRAFT - Llangynidr, Monmouthshire & Brecon Canal, Map 45. Tel: 01874 730850. www.country-craft.co.uk

COUNTRYWIDE CRUISERS - Brewood, Shropshire Union Canal, Map 2. Tel; 01902 850166. www.countrywide-cruisers.com

EMPRESS HOLIDAYS - Nantwich, Shropshire Union Canal, Map 11. Tel: 01270 624075. www.empressholidays.com

CHAS HARDERN - Beeston, Shropshire Union Canal, Map13. Tel: 01829 732595. www.chashardern.co.uk

MAESTERMYN HIRE CRUISERS - Whittington, Llangollen Canal, Map 24. Tel: 01691 662424. www.maestermyn.co.uk

MARINE CRUISES - Chirk, Llangollen Canal, Map 25. Tel: 01691 774558. www.chirkmarina.com

MIDDLEWICH NARROWBOATS - Middlewich, Trent & Mersey Canal, Map 29. Tel: 01606 832460. www.middlewichboats.co.uk

NORBURY WHARF - Norbury Junction, Shropshire Union Canal, Map 5.Tel: 01785 284292.

RED LINE BOATS - Goytre Wharf, Monmouthshire & Brecon Canal, Map 41. Tel: 01873 880516. www.redlineboats.co.uk

ROAD HOUSE HIRE - Gilwern, Monmouthshire & Brecon Canal, Map 43. Tel: 01873 830240. www.narrowboats-wales.co.uk

VIKING AFLOAT - Whitchurch, Llangollen Canal, Map 20. Tel: 01905 610660. www.viking-afloat.com

WATER TRAVEL - Autherley Junction, Shropshire Union Canal, Map 1. Tel: 01902 789942. www.watertravel.co.uk

Day Boat Hire*

BRECON BOATS - Talybont-on-Usk, Monmouthshire & Brecon Canal, Map 45. Tel: 01874 676401.

MAESBURY WHARF CRUISERS - Gronwen Wharf, Montgomery Canal, Map 33. Tel: 01691 679963.

A number of the hire bases listed opposite also offer day hire.

Boatyards

BARBRIDGE MARINA - Barbridge, Shropshire Union Canal, Map 12. Tel: 01270 528682.

BLACKWATER MEADOW MARINA - Ellesmere, Llangollen Canal, Map 23. Tel: 01691 624391.

BOAT BUILDING SERVICES - Stoak, Shropshire Union Canal, Map 17. Tel: 0151 357 1949.

CHIRK MARINE - Chirk, Llangollen Canal, Map 25. Tel: 01691 774558.

HOLIDAYS AFLOAT - Market Drayton, Shropshire Union Canal, Map 8. Tel: 01630 652937.

KINGS LOCK - Middlewich, Trent & Mersey Canal, Map 29. Tel: 01606 737564.

NANTWICH CANAL CENTRE - Nantwich, Shropshire Union Canal, Map 11. Tel: 01270 625122.

ORCHARD MARINA - Northwich, Trent & Mersey Canal, Map 30. Tel: 01606 42082.

TED'S BOATYARD - Market Drayton, Shropshire Union Canal, Map 8. Tel: 01630 658282.

VENETIAN MARINE - Cholmondeston, Shropshire Union Canal Middlewich Branch, Map 12. Tel: 01270 528251.

WHIXALL MARINE - Whixall, Llangollen Canal, Map 22. Tel: 01948 880420.

WHINCHAM WHARF - Lostock Gralam, Trent & Mersey Canal, Map 31. Tel: 01606 44672.

Boating through Brewood

Information

How To Use The Maps

There are forty-seven numbered maps whose layout is shown by the Route Planner inside the front cover. Maps 1 to 17 cover the 'main line' of the Shropshire Union Canal between Autherley Junction (Wolverhampton) and Ellesmere Port; Maps18 to 27 cover the Llangollen Canal from Hurleston Junction (Nantwich) to Horseshoe Falls (Llangollen); Maps 28 to 31 cover the Middlewich Branch of the Shropshire Union together with the Trent & Mersey Canal between Middlewich and Anderton (Northwich); Maps 32 to 39 cover the Montgomery Canal from Frankton to Newtown (users should note that this canal is only partially navigable at present); Maps 40 to 47 cover the Monmouthshire & Brecon Canal from Pontnewydd (Cwmbran) to Brecon. The maps are easily read in either direction. The simplest way of progressing from map to map is to proceed to the next map numbered from the edge of the map you are on. Figures quoted at the top of each map refer to distance per map, locks per map and average cruising time. An alternative indication of timings from centre to centre can be found on the Route Planner. Obviously, cruising times vary with the nature of your boat and the number of crew at your disposal, so quoted times should be taken only as an estimate. Neither do times quoted take into account any delays which might occur at lock flights in high season.

Using The Text

Each map is accompanied by a route commentary. Regular readers will already be familiar with our somewhat irreverent approach. But we 'tell it as we find it', in the belief that the users of this guide will find this attitude more valuable than a strict adherence to the tourist publicity line: twenty-five years of research and feedback and nearly half a million sales suggest that you broadly agree!

Towpath Walking

The simplest way to go canal exploring is on foot. It costs largely nothing and you are free to concentrate on the passing scene; something that boaters are not always at liberty to do. As usual the maps show the quality of the towpath, and whilst it does vary from area to area, none of it should prove problematical for anyone inured to the vicissitudes of country walking. We recommend the use of public transport to facilitate 'one-way' itineraries but stress the advisability of checking up to date details on the telephone numbers quoted.

Towpath Cycling

Cycling canal towpaths is an increasingly popular activity, but one which British Waterways - the body responsible for the upkeep of the bulk of Britain's navigable inland waterways - is only slowly coming to terms with. At present it is necessary for cyclists wishing to use towpaths to acquire a free of charge permit from a British Waterways office - see opposite.

Boating

Boating on inland waterways is an established, though relatively small, facet of the UK holiday industry. There are over 30,000 privately owned boats registered on the canals, but in addition to these, numerous firms offer boats for hire. These range from small operators with half a dozen boats to sizeable fleets run by companies with several bases.

Most hire craft have all the creature comforts you are likely to expect. In the excitement of planning a boating holiday you may give scant thought to the contents of your hire boat, but at the end of a hard day's boating such matters take on more significance, and a well equipped, comfortable boat, large enough to accommodate your crew with something to spare, can make the difference between a good holiday and an indifferent one.

Traditionally, hire boats are booked out by the week or fortnight, though many firms now offer more flexible short breaks or extended weeks. All reputable hire firms give newcomers tuition in boat handling and lock working, and first-timers soon find themselves adapting to the pace of things.

Navigational Advice

LOCKS are part of the charm of canal cruising, but they are potentially dangerous environments for children, pets and careless adults. Use of them should be methodical and unhurried, whilst special care should be exercised in rain, frost and snow when slippery hazards abound. We lack space for detailed instructions on lock operation: trusting that if you own a boat you will, by definition, already be experienced in canal cruising; whilst first-time hire boaters should be given tuition in the operation of locks before they set out.

The majority of locks included in this guide are of the narrow variety. However, on the Shropshire Union Canal north of Nantwich they are widebeam and capable of accommodating two narrowboats side by side. There are 'staircase' locks at Bunbury, Grindley Brook and Frankton where adjacent chambers share common gates. When working uphill the upper chamber must be full so that the water in it can be released to fill the lower chamber. Going downhill, the lower chamber must be empty to enable the water from the upper chamber to flow into it.

LIFT BRIDGES are a feature of the Llangollen, Montgomery and Monmouthshire & Brecon canals. Many are now modern metal structures operated with the use of a lock windlass. There are, however, a number of original wooden built structures still operated by counter balance weights. Great care should be taken to ensure that the bridge platform remains firmly upright as your boat passes through. Lift bridges at Wrenbury (Llangollen Canal) and Talybont (Mon & Brec) are electrically operated using a British Waterways sanitary key.

MOORING on the canals featured in this guide is per usual practice - ie on the towpath side, away from sharp bends, bridge-holes and narrows. An 'open' bollard symbol represents visitor mooring sites; either as designated specifically by British Waterways or, in some cases, as recommended by our personal experience.

PRIVATE NAVIGATIONS which connect with British Waterways canals covered in this guide are the Manchester Ship Canal at Ellesmere Port (Map 17) and the River Dee at Chester (Map 16). Hire boaters will not be permitted to enter either of these waterways; private pleasure craft may use the MSC only if they comply with a number of strict conditions, such as Third Party insurance and a Certificate of Seaworthiness. Full details from the Harbour Master, Manchester Ship Canal, Queen Elizabeth II Dock, Eastham, Wirral CH62 0BB. Tel: 0151 327 1461.

The Dee below Chester is a tidal, fast flowing river not recommended for use by canal craft. The Upper Dee, however, flows charmingly through the Cheshire countryside and may be reached via the Dee Branch. Contact Chester City Council, River Patrol, Grosvenor Park Lodge, Grosvenor Park, Chester CH1 1QQ. Tel: 01244 324324.

CLOSURES (or 'stoppages' in canal parlance) traditionally occur on the inland waterways between November and April, during which time most of the heavy maintenance work is undertaken. Occasionally, however, an emergency stoppage, or perhaps water restriction, may be imposed at short notice, closing part of the route you intend to use. Up-to-date details are usually available from hire bases and British Waterways provide a recorded message on 01923 201401. Information is also available on BW's internet site at www.waterscape.com

Emergencies

British Waterways operate a central emergency telephone service. Tel: 0800 4799 947.

Useful Contacts

BRITISH WATERWAYS - Wales & Border Counties, Navigation Road, Northwich, Cheshire CW8 1BH. Tel: 01606 723800.
Monmouthshire & Brecon Canal - Canal Office, The Wharf, Govilon, Abergavenny NP7 9NY. Tel: 01873 830328.

Societies

The Inland Waterways Association was founded in 1946 to campaign for retention of the canal system. Many routes now open to pleasure boaters may not have been so but for this organisation. Membership details may be obtained from: Inland Waterways Association, PO Box 114, Rickmansworth WD3 1ZY. Tel: 01923 711114. www.waterways.org.uk

Acknowledgements

Many thanks to Brian Collings for the cover; to Toby Bryant for keeping his eyes and ears open; Karen Tanguy for proof-reading and additional research; and to all at Hawksworths of Uttoxeter who printed this edition. Mapping reproduced by permission of Ordnance Survey on behalf of Her Majesty's Stationery Office, Crown Copyright 100033032.

Nine Good Reasons for Exploring the Canals with Pearsons

7th edition - ISBN 0 9545383 9 0

8th edition - ISBN 0 9549116 0 1

7th edition - ISBN 0 9549116 3 6

7th edition - ISBN 0 9545383 8 2

5th edition - ISBN 0 907864 99 6

6th edition - ISBN 0 9545383 1 5

6th edition - ISBN 0 9549116 2 8

3rd edition - ISBN 0 9545383 4 X

1st edition - ISBN 0 907864 97 X

Pearson's Canal Companions are published by Central Waterways Supplies. They are widely available from hire bases, boatyards, canal shops, good bookshops, via the internet and the Inland Waterways Association. For further details contact CWS on 01788 546692 or sales@centralwaterways.co.uk